‘This is a heartwarming book full to the brim with love of family, of friends, of football. Yet, we discover in its pages just how much courage it takes to be true to yourself and show that love in good times and bad.’ **The Hon. Julia Gillard AC**

‘Katrina’s book is a powerful testament to grit, endurance and agility. It shows how perseverance, focus, and strong values lead to true success. A must-read for anyone seeking strength in themselves and those they love.’ **Cathy Freeman OAM**

‘This book is a valuable reminder that we never know what someone may be struggling through and kindness goes a long way. Mini has already inspired many, and reading her story gave me an even deeper admiration for the way she balances motherhood and football at the highest level.’ **Mary Fowler**

‘Katrina is an inspiration. Yes, obviously for her incredible athletic abilities, but for me what is even more inspiring is the way she unapologetically knows who she is, what she wants and then, goes after it. Even when it might not make sense to anyone else, or the path forward may seem unclear at first. A brilliant insight into one of Australia’s best.’ **Libby Trickett OAM**

‘Good things come in small packages. Katrina Gorry tells a story of resilience, of loss, of love and the unwavering determination to have the courage to carve your own path. Mini in name is not mini in heart.’ **Tara Rushton**

Katrina Gorry is a professional football player who made her debut for both the Matildas and W-League club Brisbane Roar in 2012. She made the leap to the US in 2014 with the National Women's Soccer League's FC Kansas City. She has played in some of the best leagues around the world, including for Japan's Vegalta Sendai, Norway's Avaldsnes and Vittsjo GIK in Sweden, expertly juggling football and motherhood following the birth of her daughter, Harper, in 2021, becoming the first player to have a baby while in our national football team.

Katrina, along with Harper and her partner, Clara Markstedt, then made the move to London, signing for West Ham United, where Katrina captains the team in the Women's Super League, with another mini Gorry in tow after the birth of their son, Koby.

Katrina was awarded 2014 AFC Women's Player of the Year and FFA Women's Player of the Year. She represented Australia in the 2015 FIFA World Cup, the 2016 Olympics, the 2014 and 2018 AFC Asian Cup, the 2019 World Cup and the immensely successful 2023 World Cup in Australia and New Zealand, where she topped the table for the most tackles, as well as the 2024 Olympics.

@katrinagorry10

KATRINA GORRY

with ROBERT WAINWRIGHT

A **Matilda's** story of football, motherhood and breaking down barriers

ALLEN&UNWIN
SYDNEY • MELBOURNE • AUCKLAND • LONDON

First published in 2025

Allen & Unwin
Cammeraygal Country
83 Alexander Street
Crows Nest NSW 2065
Australia
Phone: (61 2) 8425 0100
Email: info@allenandunwin.com
Web: www.allenandunwin.com

Allen & Unwin acknowledges the Traditional Owners of the Country on which we live and work. We pay our respects to all Aboriginal and Torres Strait Islander Elders, past and present.

A catalogue record for this book is available from the National Library of Australia

ISBN 978 1 76147 216 9

Except where otherwise stated, all photographs are from the author's collection
Set in 12/18 pt Sabon LT Pro by Midland Typesetters, Australia
Printed and bound in Australia by the Opus Group

10 9 8 7 6 5 4 3 2 1

The paper in this book is FSC® certified. FSC® promotes environmentally responsible, socially beneficial and economically viable management of the world's forests.

To my family
The most important team

CONTENTS

PROLOGUE

The Numbers Game

It wouldn't be much of a football team if everyone was the same type of player, would it?

We need agile goalkeepers, resolute defenders, nippy midfielders, pacy wingers, tall forwards and instinctive strikers. There must be speedsters and chasers, tacklers and dribblers, passers and headers, and savers and scorers.

A successful team is made of eleven individuals whose on-field roles and relationships have traditionally been defined by our jersey numbers—the goalkeeper is always number 1, fullbacks wear 2 and 3, centre backs 4 and 5, defensive midfielder 6, wingers 7 and 11, central midfielder 8, and striker 9.

In my junior days I wore number 10, which signifies chief playmaker and attacking midfielder, but when I moved into senior teams I had to start again and work my way up through the ranks.

Other numbers creep into the game depending on the size of the squad. Number 13 was my first jersey when I joined Melbourne Victory as a seventeen-year-old and played off the bench. I got the number 8 jersey at Adelaide United the following year, and played as an attacking midfielder whose job was to score goals but also provide a link between attack and defence.

By the time I joined my home club Brisbane Roar a few seasons later I was given the coveted number 10 shirt because I had become a more senior and successful player.

When I was selected to play for the Matildas in 2012, I was back at the bottom of the heap. The number 10 jersey was taken so I decided to do the next best thing and show my desire to improve. I chose number 19 because 1 + 9 = 10. Over the years since, I have often played the number 10 role depending on the team structure and tactics.

In 2024 things changed again when I went to the Olympics with the Matildas. It was my first Olympics since my daughter Harper's arrival and I now wore the number 6 jersey, which not only was Clara's playing number, but also signified my adjusted role in the team as a defensive midfielder or, as then coach Tony Gustavsson described it, the team's quarterback.

I have been described as 'a whirring, bustling ball of metronomic energy in the centre of the park'. It makes me happy to be seen that way because that is how I see myself, as a player prepared to run and run and run for the team.

Individual goals are a joyous moment, but so too is making a tackle to turn the ball over, or setting up a goal through a chain of passes.

I love sprinting back as fast as I can to make a tackle, to exert myself to a new level. I even tried to push myself in one match to get cramp because I hadn't experienced the burning sensation before, which made me feel as if I wasn't working hard enough. When I finally got a cramp, my groin seized up and I couldn't walk after the match. I remember thinking, 'Ah, so that's what everyone is talking about.'

But I am more than a footballer.

I am a mother. I am a partner, a daughter and a sister. I am gay. I am small and I am Australian. I am fierce. I am loyal. I love my family and my friends. I can be funny and cheeky, but I can also be vulnerable and emotional.

These are all the things that make up me, as Coco Chanel once wrote: 'A girl should be two things: who and what she wants.'

It's a bit strange that I'm quoting a fashion designer, given that my favourite outfit is a tracksuit and I hate dressing up, but her observation sums up the most important things in a person's existence—their identity and ambitions.

They are such powerful words but so full of complexities.

I was christened Katrina-Lee, not for any particular reason other than Mum liked the name Katrina and hyphenated names. The name Katrina-Lee appeared on some of my early team sheets and archived match results, but these days I don't use it.

The reason? Because that's the name that Mum would use if I was in trouble, which was fairly often when I was a teenager: 'Katrina-Lee, what have you done? Katrina-Lee, get in here. Katrina-Lee, where are you?' You get the idea.

I don't see myself as particularly rebellious or naughty but I have always tended to push boundaries, particularly when someone tells me I can't do something. It becomes a challenge—'Yeah, well I'll show you.' It began as a child when I was told that girls can't play football.

It probably got me into a bit of trouble as a teenager, at school and with my parents. But I'm older and more mature now and tend to make wiser decisions about what to challenge and why. I pick my fights a little better now. Although some people, including my dad, Peter, would say that I still need to learn a little discipline on the field. I have been known to get a little feisty on the pitch, most notably during the pressure and emotion of the World Cup matches in 2023.

Most of the time I'm known at home as Trine or Trina, while friends call me Mini because at 154 centimetres (five foot one inch), I am small. It doesn't bother me. Never really has. Rather, it has been a driving force in my life inspiring me to achieve more than people think I can achieve.

Several coaches told me that I was too small to ever be selected to play for the Matildas, and at the time of writing this I've played 107 matches in national colours.

There has always been another burning desire in my life. I told my family and friends when I was thirteen years old that I wanted to be a mum and do it by myself. It was a strange thing for someone so young to say. Most women want a wedding and a partner and security, but I wanted to do it on my own because I'd decided that I didn't need anybody else. I'm not sure that I fully believed that back then but, when the time came, that's what actually happened.

But then my identity evolved again. I unexpectedly fell in love with a Swedish girl and, suddenly, the teenager who didn't need anyone now wanted to share her world and life with a partner. Not only that, but we had another child, Koby, so now we are four.

I grew up with eight brothers and sisters—well, seven brothers and one sister to be exact. I once told my stepmother, Michelle, that I loved being in a big family because I could always find someone to play with, but family is more significant than that to me. I have my family members' names tattooed on my body because they mean so much to me. I love their company and their support; I love their similarities and adore their differences.

My parents, Linda and Peter, still follow me to virtually every match I play. It's not because they live and breathe my wins and losses (although they do) but because they are proud of their daughter and who I am.

These are some of the things that make me who I am. This is me.

CHAPTER ONE

My Backyard Beginnings

I didn't grow up with sporting heroes. There were no posters of idols on my bedroom walls and no football on television in rugby league–mad Brisbane when I was a kid during the 1990s.

Instead, my inspirations for the game were my older brothers, Daniel and Joel. I idolised them. And when they played for the Mansfield Eagles in our local church league, I followed their every move from the sidelines.

From the age of five or six I demanded to be included in my brothers' backyard kickabouts. We'd spar in rough and tumble one-on-one contests, dodging beneath the Hills hoist washing line and around the cubbyhouse, all the while avoiding our leaping, barking cattle dog, Legend, who was an extra defender as we tried to score. The goals were usually marked by two old shoes.

There was no such thing as fouls—you just wore the bumps and scratches if you were shoved or knocked over—and when we weren't scrapping, playing one-v-one and giving each other 'bummies' (kicking the ball into each other's backsides as punishment for letting in goals) then we had juggling competitions, trying to keep the ball in the air, or the boys were teaching me tricks.

It was football as it should be—fun and inclusive. I lost count of the number of windows we broke in those years, although I'm sure Mum probably remembers. I was always getting into trouble for playing with a football inside the house, and even slept with a ball because I was so obsessed with the game.

Daniel was the quiet one, a dependable and smart centre back who was a good tackler, whereas Joel was a more mercurial and skilful player, always testing boundaries. He loved doing the rainbow, where he back-heeled the ball behind his body and over my head to rub in how short I was.

I'd retaliate by deliberately annoying him to exploit his short fuse. I knew if I pressed his buttons that sooner or later it would set him off. Daniel and I would end up hiding in a room, giggling at the joke while Joel chased us with a mop.

Disagreements, arguments and even the occasional scrap were inevitable, but I gave as good as I got. If things threatened to get out of hand then my older sister, Amanda, would end up refereeing, settling everyone down and picking up the pieces, especially after school when she was boss until Mum got home from work.

I can only remember one occasion when things got a bit willing between Daniel and Joel and they ended up chasing each other around the streets. Eventually they wrestled themselves, bare chested, into a cactus bush, and emerged dripping with blood.

But the disagreements were boisterous rather than serious, never lasting long and undoubtedly making us stronger, individually and as a group, because we always made up and got along with one another afterwards—like a good team.

Looking back, this childhood bonding helped me understand what it meant to be part of a team, where you can have influence on others as well as being influenced by them before you all move in a direction together. I don't think I would have done as well in an individual sport because I needed to belong in a group and have others—team-mates—around me. It's why loyalty is so important to me; a commitment to others as well as yourself.

As a midfielder, you are the team's engine room and you can see the game differently to others, steering the ship in another direction if needs be. That's who I am: not a captain so much as an on-field manager.

I think I learned about that from Amanda. She was seven years older than me and yet, even as a teenager with her own friends, she always looked out for the rest of us and kept me and the boys safe and in line whenever Mum and Dad weren't around.

She was the unifying force and led by example, whether it was re-establishing peace in backyard football or calling an end to the hijinks when it was time to come inside and get on with our homework.

I loved our first family home in Frampton Street, Alexandra Hills, Brisbane. I can still picture it in my head, a big palm tree out the front and a hill where we'd race our bikes. I once crashed while being 'dinked' and shredded my foot in the spokes. When Dad tried to disinfect the wound with Dettol, the pain was even worse. I still have the scars. It was a dangerous bit of road when I think about it because Joel once stacked it, face first on his skateboard, and tore his mouth and nose badly. But we all took these childhood injuries in our stride.

There was bushland at the bottom of the street where my brothers and I played nearly every day. When we weren't kicking a ball, we were creating trails with jumps to race our bikes or building cubbies and capturing insects. Mum's only rule was to be home by sundown.

The house was split level, the ground floor consisted of a big lounge room off the front entrance with the kitchen and dining room at the back. Upstairs, above the garage, there were four bedrooms. Amanda, being the oldest, had a room to herself, Daniel and Joel shared a bedroom as did I with my younger brother Lachlan when he arrived five years after me.

The layout of the house meant that Daniel, Joel and I could hide at the top of the stairs at night and peer over Mum's and Dad's shoulders below as they sat on the couch watching television.

If we were quiet then we could sit there unseen, thrilled that we could watch programs like *Law & Order*, which would otherwise have been expressly forbidden. If Mum and Dad knew we were there then they never let on. If I hadn't become a professional footballer, I wanted to be a police officer. I've always liked the idea of solving puzzles and admired people who have the sleuthing skills to sniff out leads. I read crime books as a kid and am a fan of Michael Connelly novels and his main hero, LAPD Detective Hieronymus Bosch.

Weekends were a time of mad chaos to get all of us kids to our sporting matches. There was mostly football for me and the boys while Amanda and Mum, who had been a decent athlete, played netball. Dad was the family bus driver, having been a very good rugby league player in his youth, spending much of his junior days playing with the great Wally Lewis. He was also a champion swimmer at school.

We spent our holidays camping in tents alongside the dingoes of Fraser Island, now known as K'gari, where we played beach football and climbed the highest sandhills to risk our necks and go tobogganing on bits of cardboard. I adored sleeping in a tent beneath a sky full of stars.

In the mornings we fished, inevitably competing against one another for the biggest catch, while the evenings were spent scouring the wide beaches, hunting for pipi shellfish to use as bait the next day.

We went to Citipointe Church most Sundays, which was a big part of our lives, stemming from a terrible car accident many years before which almost killed Dad's parents. He was a teenager at the time and their survival strengthened his family's faith in the church.

Dad and Mum were already childhood sweethearts at that time and she was going through her own trauma as her father battled cancer. The church provided her with some comfort when he passed away soon afterwards.

Our lives changed dramatically when I was nine years old and Mum and Dad divorced. The house had to go and Mum took us kids and moved south to the outer suburb of Belmont where the backyard football games with my brothers were a comforting constant in an otherwise pretty mixed-up time as we tried to re-establish our lives.

I realise that divorce is a reality for many marriages, but as a kid who adored being part of a big family, the concept of Dad having to move out didn't make any sense to me. I thought he had simply gone away for a while, for a holiday or work or something, and then he would come back. But he didn't.

I don't remember our parents ever arguing in front of us. They had met each other when they were teenagers and I guess they just grew apart. I never asked at the time because I was probably too afraid to hear the answer and it doesn't really matter now as life has moved on.

It wasn't a terrible divorce, as divorces go. There was no anger, as far as I remember, but it still felt like our world had been shattered and it left a mark on me that has driven probably the most important decision in my life—becoming a single mum.

For a long time afterwards I couldn't envisage bringing a child into the world in partnership with someone else because of the risk of splitting up and putting my child through the same experience. That is not a comment on my parents' situation—they made the decision they believed was right—but I found it difficult to trust relationships as a result. Thankfully, those feelings have passed and having met and married Clara, I now believe in love, and forever after.

Even though they were divorced, Mum and Dad always had a civil relationship and worked hard together in the early years to manage our lives, and in particular our sport. Our house with Mum in Belmont was bigger than our old house so I got my own room.

Both Mum and Dad found new partners. Mum lives with David, my stepfather, and Dad married my stepmum, Michelle. Both David and Michelle have been very important parts of my life and great supporters.

Apparently I was the matchmaker between Dad and Michelle. They had met at a Christmas party organised by the church and, according to Michelle, Dad had come home that night and told us about a woman in a red dress. (Michelle is proud of that dress, which she bought at the Salvos—'The best twenty dollars I ever spent,' she reckons.)

The next Sunday, Michelle remembers me waiting for her when she arrived at church. I whispered, 'Here she comes, Dad,' as she tried to hide her embarrassment. After the service I went up to her to introduce myself. She assumed that I wanted to cuddle her son Jared who was a year old but, no, I wanted to organise a coffee date between her and Dad, pretending it was his idea when it was mine.

The rest, as they say, is history. Michelle and Dad got together, despite her initial reticence at becoming involved with a divorced man with five children. Michelle brought three boys of her own to the relationship, my stepbrothers Eden, Morgan and Jared.

I happened to be playing a game for the Mansfield Eagles on the morning of Dad and Michelle's wedding in 2002. It was arranged that Mum would drop me at the Sheraton Hotel in the city where Michelle and her bridesmaids were getting ready so I could get changed. The invitations went out for a 2 pm ceremony followed by a reception for one hundred guests.

About a week before the wedding I was told that my match would start later, but rather than pull out of the team I implored Dad to put back the ceremony and reception by an hour so I could play. When he and Michelle questioned whether an under tens match should have priority over a wedding for which the guests had already RSVP'd, I insisted: 'I can't let the team down.'

I was so fixated on playing that Dad and Michelle sighed and agreed. I can only imagine their embarrassment at having to contact their guests and tell them to come an hour later, and when asked why, having to explain that it was only because of Katrina's football game. I'm caught between giggling and cringing when I think about it now.

It was getting late when I finally arrived at the hotel. Michelle looked shocked when she saw me, still in my boots and muddy from head to toe. 'You'll need a shower,' she said, looking me up and down. Thankfully we got to the ceremony in time with me transformed from muddy football urchin into pretty flower girl.

After trying to juggle Christmas for a few years, Mum and Dad decided to spend Christmas mornings together with all the kids, as well as Michelle and David. It wasn't an easy thing to do but they were able to put their differences aside to ensure that us kids came first.

Christmas was always a joyful and noisy affair which traditionally started with Mum and David making breakfast for the mob and 'Santa' turning up to hand out presents for all the kids. We used to take it in turns to play Santa but one year, when it was my turn, my younger brother Dylan insisted that I must be the real Santa so I was stuck with the role, including wearing the itchy beard.

We've all grown up now but we still have Christmas morning together, and with so many grandchildren we had to introduce Santa's helpers to clear the sea of presents beneath the tree.

There was another aspect of Christmas that I enjoyed. Dad was a truck driver for the Brisbane Ice Works and would spend the week before Christmas delivering ice around the city to various shops. It was an early morning start in the summer heat and Dad encouraged me and my brothers to go with him to help haul the bags out from the truck freezer, and he would then load them into the ice machines.

Dad remembers me being so small that he would sling me into the back of the truck after we arrived at a shop so I could climb the wall of ice, stacked in 5-kilogram and 10-kilogram bags, and throw or roll them down to him. Joel and I would compete to see who could keep their hand in the ice the longest and we all earned a bit of pocket money for our troubles. But the bit I liked best was sitting in the truck talking to Dad. Those conversations were about nothing in particular but everything in terms of what life is about.

I have a tattoo on my right ankle of an infinity symbol with the name Dylan. Dylan is Dad and Michelle's son and my beloved brother. The symbol refers to the link that Dylan's birth in December 2002 created—the joining together of the two halves of my family—and its importance in my life.

It was probably my pestering which led to his arrival. I kept hammering Dad and Michelle to have a baby to complete the family circle. I wouldn't have blamed them if they'd ignored me, given that Jared was under two years old and Morgan, although a few years older, is severely disabled and requires around-the-clock care.

It meant that every second weekend when the rest of us went to Dad's house, there were eight kids demanding attention. Dylan made nine—a Brady Bunch without the luxury of Alice, the housekeeper.

To me it was heaven when Dylan was born, because not only did I have Jared and Morgan to carry around but a new baby to cuddle. Apparently, when I stayed at Dad's house, I not only changed Dylan's nappies but often used to sleep on the floor next to his cot.

Dylan was born with Down Syndrome. It makes him special rather than different. I remember talking to Michelle about how it would affect his life and her answer was simply that he would learn to do things at his own pace, a little slower than the rest of us, but he would still do most things that the rest of us could do.

If I think back on it, his birth must have been quite devastating for Michelle, given that she already had the challenges of looking after Morgan. In those early moments, it would have been hard to see through the difficulties that special needs children bring, particularly as she was starting a new relationship with my father in a large and complex family.

But those feelings quickly disappeared because Dylan is the glue that bonded our new, expanded family. It meant that we all grew up knowing and accepting that everyone is an individual. Michelle once tried to explain to Lachy and Eden that Dylan had Down Syndrome, and they responded: 'No, he doesn't!' They objected to the idea that his difference meant he wasn't the same as them, as they knew he was just as good as everybody else.

One of my favourite memories is being at Dylan's school one Christmas and watching him and his classmates' Christmas presentation. They were singing carols and dancing around the stage, their smiles so wide I thought their faces would split. They were the epitome of pure joy and an inspiring reminder that we should all live in the moment and enjoy the simple pleasures of life.

I loved looking up into the stands during a Roar match and seeing Dylan sitting there with his headphones and iPad, enjoying the atmosphere even though he finds loud noises difficult. He can't help but mingle and occasionally flirt with the girls afterwards and has even proposed to my team-mate and great friend Michelle Heyman.

Dylan helped make me braver and fairer as a human being. There was a special class at my high school and some of the boys could be very cruel. I'm sure it was because of my experiences with Dylan and Morgan, but I found myself feeling as if I had to be these kids' protector whenever there was a problem.

There was one boy who couldn't stand people clapping their hands and I found him one day screaming because he was surrounded by a bunch of boys clapping in his face. I got so angry that I pushed one of them off a table. It just broke my heart because the boy had been brave enough to come to school and didn't deserve to be treated that way.

There was a young girl who had what looked like burns all over her body. I don't know why she was in the special education unit but she was constantly being teased in the playground and scratched at herself in anxiety. If I saw it happen, I would take her over to our group of girls so she could sit with us.

I was having a conversation with Harper recently about this. We were on a train in Sweden when I noticed her looking quizzically at a young woman with disabilities, as if she was trying to figure her out: 'You know, not everyone is the same,' I told her. 'There are all sorts of people in the world and we have to accept them for who they are.'

Harper looked at me as if I was an idiot. 'I know,' she replied. I realised then that she wasn't casting judgement, just trying to place the young woman in context.

I think that's the key. There is a place for everyone in this world, like in a football team. I can't imagine our family without Dylan and the joy he brings because he is who he is.

CHAPTER TWO

If a Shoe Doesn't Fit, Wear It Anyway

I have what you might call a stubborn streak. At times, the term pig-headed might have been more appropriate, like the year I began primary school at Citipointe Christian College, in Carindale. I had set my heart on a certain teacher—Mrs Smith—who was a favourite of my older brothers. Instead I was put in the other class with a teacher I didn't know.

I was so outraged by the injustice of it all that I decided to go on strike. That way they'd have to put me in the class with Mrs Smith, or so I thought. The standoff lasted almost the first half of the school year, with me refusing to be taught and the school refusing to bow down to the demands of a belligerent six-year-old.

It got to the point that the school principal told Mum that I would most likely have to repeat the year if I didn't start co-operating. I eventually relented, and by the end of the year I thought the teacher was actually quite nice.

On other occasions, my stubbornness has worked in my favour, like my entry into football. Mum wanted me to play netball, the sport she and Amanda played. Besides, everyone said back then, girls don't play football.

But I was insistent that football was my game. I had been kicking a ball with my brothers almost since I could walk and the idea of playing throw and catch with other girls was, well, *boring*. That's what I told Mum as we drove to the courts the first morning to register with the nippers netball competition, but it was like talking to a brick wall.

I remember angrily getting out of the car and telling her that I didn't want to play netball. I wasn't interested. Mum registered me anyway.

When I was put on the court to play centre, I promptly sat down in protest. I got up grudgingly when play started but as soon as the ball came to me, I booted it off the court.

Unsurprisingly, I was taken off. Mum was so embarrassed, but thankfully she also saw the light. 'I'm not going to put up with this every weekend. Okay, I get it. You can play football.' And that was that.

The next week Mum signed me up to play for the Mansfield Eagles in the local church league. The only problem was that the club did not have a girls' team, so I would have to play with the boys. It made no difference to me. I was used to playing with my brothers.

From the moment I ran onto the ground, I loved the experience. I was now part of a team with uniforms (so big they seemed to swallow me) on a playing field, with a referee with a whistle and parents watching and yelling from the sidelines. It was a real game, not just imagined or kicking around in the backyard with a dog and a clothesline for opposition. I was where I wanted to be and I loved the atmosphere.

There is a photograph of me at that time. My hair is up and I'm giving the camera a bucktooth grin. But my apparent shyness hid a toughness I'd learned from playing backyard football with Daniel and Joel. My secret weapon, even at that age, was tackling, particularly at right back where I initially played. I loved the slide tackle, the idea of sweeping the ball from beneath the feet of my opponents and watching the surprise on their faces, as well as on the faces of the opposition coaches and parents.

But life is never as simple as it should be, and it wasn't long before some of those parents began to object to their sons 'being beaten by a girl'. I could hear the comments from the field. At first it was confusing. I was an easy target, a tiny girl in an oversized shirt. But rather than being upset by their comments, it motivated me to wipe the smirks off their faces and make them really sorry.

And I did.

I was triumphant in one early match when my tackle freed the ball and my team-mates pounced on it, took the ball to the other end of the ground and scored a goal. It may have seemed like an insignificant moment in a junior match at some obscure suburban ground but the memory has stayed with me over the years; an early vindication that I belonged and I could hold my own, despite what others might think.

Luckily for me, our coach Bruce Irwin was as interested in teaching us about enjoying the game as he was about winning. Bruce, who was also a family friend, made it a point to ensure I felt that I belonged out there on the pitch with the boys, even though I was one of just a handful of girls in the competition and the only one on our team. Bruce told me I shouldn't worry about what others said and did. It was exactly what I needed to hear.

There would be many such incidents as I got older and moved to a different club and league where I was still playing against the boys. Dad remembers one boy—a bit of a bully—coming off the ground at half-time and telling his team-mates, 'Don't let a girl get in front of you; get the ball off her and send it to me.' I apparently overheard the remark and spent the second half running rings around the boy, much to his embarrassment and fury.

Mum says that even some of the opposition team parents reacted badly to my presence on the field, catcalling during one match that I 'didn't belong on the ground', which prompted an objection from our team's parents. The two groups started arguing and the situation quickly descended into pushing and shoving before thankfully being resolved.

It's pathetic that in this day and age men would still teach their sons that women are weak and inferior.

Rather than be upset by this blatant misogyny, I used it as a spur to succeed, and my revenge was sweet. When I was ten years old we attended a state-wide church football carnival after which an 'honorary' Queensland team was selected. There were 125 boys and one girl in contention for selection, and the first name called out was mine.

When I was nine I joined my first girls' team, playing in the under-12s for the Mount Gravatt Hawks in the Brisbane Metro League. Our coach Andy trained us on Friday evenings and loved teaching us ball skills and tricks.

Training sessions were fun and challenging rather than arduous, teaching us the skill foundations we needed to be able to concentrate on the tactics of the game as we got older and progressed through the juniors and into the ranks of senior football. Typically there were exercises to encourage us to use our non-preferred foot and to perfect our dribbling skills and work on other moves like stepovers, the scissors, the drag back, the Cruyff turn and the rainbow flick that Joel loved so much. Andy encouraged us to use these skills not only in training but in match situations.

I loved training and would go home and practise and practise until I got the week's challenge right. When we went back the next week Andy handed out lollies or other prizes to whoever did the move best.

'Katrina always won the lollies,' Mum remembers.

Around this time, the signs that I could have a future in the game were becoming more frequent and obvious, especially to Mum.

'People kept saying, "You know, your daughter has got something; she could be special." We'd go to some district games and there'd be people on the sidelines—talent spotters—watching the girls.

'There she was, this tiny thing in a pale blue, one-size-fits-all representative team uniform. The shirts fell to her forearms and the shorts way past her knees. Once her socks had been pulled up, the only flesh you could see was her face.

'But it didn't seem to matter. It was her attitude to the game and her ball skills that made her stand out. All those Friday night sessions and hours of practising at home meant she was something different.

'One year at a Brisbane Southern Districts game, when she was about twelve, this guy came up and told us that Katrina had been earmarked as a player of the future and they were going to keep an eye on her development over the next few years. As parents, all you could do was go along with the flow and do whatever was needed to give her that chance.

'Being small made no difference to Katrina. If anything, it probably made her more determined. One year she entered the cross-country race at her school, which she won, and went on to the zone championships where the kids were bigger and stronger. She came last in the race, a long way behind the others and I remember watching some of the other parents pointing fingers and laughing that she wasn't up to it.

'Katrina's response was not to get upset but to try again. She won the school race again the next year and went to the zone finals. This time she came sixth. It was a victory that she could respond to the challenge rather than give up and stop trying. I was very proud of her.'

Mum was also very keen that I didn't get ahead of myself and kept a level head. 'Just be confident and don't be cocky', was her mantra. It was damn good advice and I've tried to follow it my entire life. Even when I made it to the Matildas I was keen to take the attitude that I had earned my spot on the team, but I had to work to keep it, because there are lots of girls with plenty of talent who would love to take my place.

My childhood obsession for football was accompanied by a desire to have the best gear. While other girls may have wanted makeup or dresses, all I was interested in was football gear and, above all, the best boots. I always wanted to have the latest and the best.

I can happily play in any kit and kick any type of ball as long as it's pumped up, but spending ninety minutes running around a football pitch means my feet need protecting.

I know that people with large feet can have trouble finding shoes that fit but the same applies to small people like me. I take size five as an adult and when I was a kid, I struggled to find a pair of boots that weren't too big for me, simply because manufacturers didn't make them small enough.

My dream shop was not a big chain store or supermarket but Football World, an unassuming suburban store in Mt Gravatt with its equally unassuming owner, Sid Camilio, who stocked anything and everything, including racks and racks of football boots.

I would insist that Mum take me there every other week in the hope of finding boots that would fit me. I was forever pretending that the ones I eventually chose were snug enough for my tiny feet even though I'd pack the front of the boot with cottonwool balls to stop them flapping, which doesn't sound terrible except that I have always despised the feeling of cottonwool.

I was twelve years old when Adidas brought out the F50 Spiderman boots. I had to have them and would go from store to store around Brisbane trying to find them in my size, all to no avail. Eventually I convinced Mum to buy a pair of men's size 6 that required not only the dreaded cottonwool but extra thick socks. I loved them. They were black with blue stitching patterned like a spiderweb and laces that tucked in with a Velcro cover. I guess you could say that I had big boots to fill from a young age.

A few years later, Lotto brought out the laceless boot and I was equally obsessed. Even now I get excited when Nike brings out their latest range. And, thanks to sponsorship by manufacturers, I can now have them tailored to fit me. It's amazing how long it has taken for manufacturers to realise that men and women are built differently and that not everyone is tall and skinny.

The amount of money Mum spent at Football World over the years was a joke. I took advantage of the fact that, when it came to football, she would never say 'no'. I'd tell her that I needed to go to the shop for a new set of shin pads when she knew damn well that I really wanted to try on new boots. If my younger brother Lachy needed new boots then I'd make sure I went along as well.

And all the while, Sid stood back and watched with a big grin on his face.

CHAPTER THREE

Coming Out

Schoolyards can be cruel places for kids like me who were a bit different from the norm.

I copped a fair amount of bullying, especially at high school. I was small and an easy target for some of the boys, particularly those who couldn't stand it when I challenged them on the sporting field. I was a tomboy with strong arms and muscular legs. I can't count the number of times I was called a man as an insult.

For the most part, I brushed off the comments and used them to inspire me to succeed, but it would have been impossible not to be impacted by the frequent negative references, particularly as I struggled through the teenage years with all their confusion and anxiety.

In my desire not to be cowed, I would go to school—Cavendish Road High School—with different haircuts in different colours, mostly copying my older sister, Amanda. She always looked cool sporting these short haircuts while I ended up walking out of the hairdresser's looking like a pineapple. I wanted to show people that I was proud of who I was, and it was important to me to feel strong.

I wasn't a bad student and always did my homework, but school wasn't my priority and my mind was usually elsewhere. I didn't like wearing my school uniform and would much rather put on my sports clothes and be outside kicking a ball with my mates.

Like most teenagers, I was wrestling with my self-identity and where I was going in life. Whatever I did, I knew it had to involve football which, by then, I pretty much lived and breathed.

My situation was complicated by the fact that I knew I was gay. It wasn't really talked about when I was a kid so I couldn't confide in anyone except my closest friends who were supportive.

Instead, I went out with a few of the boys, trying to please people around me, even though I knew that I really wasn't interested in dating them. They were just friends, but the act made me appear like everyone else. It just shows the conflict within me at the time between my natural defiance and a teenager's desire to fit in.

I didn't start going out with girls until I was in my late teens. By then I'd left school and found the safety and security of women's football where there is greater acceptance of different sexualities and it was easier to be myself.

There is a wide perception that all women footballers are gay. It isn't true although it *is* true that there is an over-representation of gay and bisexual women in the game. That is partly due to the fact that women's football is more welcoming, diverse and open than many other sports where tribalism is still a major factor.

At the 2019 Women's World Cup, for example, there were forty-one players and coaches who were openly gay compared to zero declared in the men's competition. There are only a handful of male footballers who have come out, although no one seriously suggests that there aren't many more still fearful of speaking out.

My home life hadn't made being gay easy either.

Dad and Michelle attended Citipointe Church, and although the church was a part of our lives and we went to services regularly when I was young, I never really felt that I was accepted because I knew that the church had a negative attitude to gay people.

Dad has been welcoming and loving towards Clara, but when she rang him to ask for his blessing to marry me, he said he wouldn't give it due to his beliefs. That felt like rejection and was hard to take—but Dad is entitled to his beliefs like we all are. I am just grateful that Dad told her in that conversation that he would always love and accept her.

I was seventeen years old when I told my mother that I was gay. I had known for a while but had always put off discussing it with my parents, not because I was afraid to do so—I have always been proud of who I am—but because I thought there was no need to 'come out', as such.

I suppose I had hoped that they would have already seen who I was, and I expected their response to be unconditional love and understanding. The reality was very different.

My conversation with Mum happened accidentally one night while she and I were sitting on the couch watching television. There was an advertisement about same-sex couples which upset me (I can't remember why). I voiced my objection and felt Mum turn towards me.

'Why are you offended?' she asked.

The words just popped out: 'Because I'm gay.'

I dared not look at her but I could tell that Mum was surprised.

'No, you're not.' Her voice was sharp.

'I am. You've always known,' I insisted.

Mum shook her head, in denial.

'No, Katrina, you feel gay because you hang out with the football girls and that's how it is.'

Mum wanted to believe it was just a phase I was going through and that I would eventually get over it, find a man and get married.

I was getting upset now.

'If you want me to be happy then you have to accept how I feel.'

My relationship with Mum was pretty normal in terms of teenagers and their mothers. We had our disagreements, arguments and even shouting matches where one of us would stalk off fuming, but it was always momentary and retrievable.

But this felt different, something deeper which really upset me. She was my mother and there should be no question when it came to my happiness. I couldn't understand why she didn't accept who I was without question.

It would take a while for us to work it out, and over the next few years Mum would be particularly hard on some of the girlfriends I brought home. She was right in many ways—some of my girlfriends were not right for me—but I'm not sure she would have been as opinionated if I was bringing boys home to meet her.

Although it's hard to write about these things, they were my genuine feelings at the time and it would be disingenuous to pretend otherwise. I know there are many young people out there today who have problems dealing with family about their sexuality.

I do not question for one moment my mum's and dad's love and devotion, only that it is important for parents to put aside generational divides when their children express different views on things like sexuality and individuality. It doesn't change who we are if we are different, and happiness is such a difficult thing to find.

I couldn't have achieved what I've done playing football and being a single mum without my own mother and her sacrifices and encouragement. And I'm happy to say that she immediately knew that Clara was the right partner for me when I brought her home.

My closest friend since childhood is Jade Saunders. We met playing football when we were ten or eleven years old and immediately hit it off. We are the same height and look so similar that people think we're sisters or even twins. To make things even more confusing, our mothers have the same birthday.

When we were young people often asked if we were related. At first we said no, but after a while we'd just nod our heads and agree because it wasn't worth explaining and, besides, we're as close as sisters can be. We ended up going to the same high school and my mum became a surrogate parent to Jade when she tragically lost both her parents, first her mum to cancer and then her dad to a heart attack two years later. I think our bond grew stronger because of the tragedies.

There are aspects to our characters which are very different, and I must admit that I took advantage of Jade a bit when we were kids. In a nice way, I hasten to add. I was much more outgoing and cheeky, unafraid of authority and confident of who I was. Jade was a little more reserved, wanting to do the right thing and avoid trouble, but she was easily roped into some of my hijinks. Whenever she hesitated, I'd just call her a goody-two-shoes, which generally did the trick.

One of those occasions was when we were about thirteen and I decided that I wanted to get my tongue pierced. As usual, I was copying my sister Amanda. I'd already got my ears and belly button pierced, and would later add my lip, but the tongue was a risk because I knew that Mum would flip out if she knew.

I'll let Jade take over the story.

'It's amazing how persuasive Mini could be, a cheeky rebel always looking for a challenge and with no fear of authority, whether it was wearing sports gear instead of school uniforms or getting out early with forged notes from our parents.

'One day after school she announced that we were going to get our tongues pierced. There was no way I was going to do it but, as usual, I followed along and, sure enough, she persuaded someone at a body piercing clinic to do it, even though she was clearly underage and the ID she flashed would have looked bogus on any serious inspection.

'Afterwards, we went back to her place where her mum had bought us Kentucky Fried Chicken for dinner. We sat down to eat and I looked over and noticed that Katrina was clearly in pain from the piercing. She was trying to hide her discomfort but her eyes were watering and Linda eventually noticed that something was amiss.

'"What's wrong Katrina?"

'"Nothing," Mini replied, sounding like her mouth was full of cottonwool, as if she'd been to the dentist.

'But Linda wasn't satisfied. "Yes, there is. You're acting really weird."

'Mini was defiant: "Nothing, Mum."

'Linda's tone changed. "I know something's wrong. Katrina, *what* have you done? Come here!"

'Mini stood up and Linda grabbed her chin and forced open her mouth to discover the piercing. It was hilarious.

'"Your tongue. What happened to your tongue? For heaven's sake, Katrina. You'll be the death of me."'

It's funny how memories can be innocently altered, subtly and even combining two incidents as one. I remember the tongue piercing slightly differently from Jade, and that I escaped detection that night but got caught out in the car on the way to school a few days later.

On reflection though, I think Jade is probably right and my memory was of the time I got my lip pierced and kept taking the ring out when I was around Mum so she wouldn't know. Then one morning I forgot to take it out and jumped in the car with her, covering my mouth with my hand when I realised my mistake. But she knew me too well, realised that I was being secretive and pulled my hand away to reveal the gold ring. I must have driven her crazy by constantly pushing the boundaries.

The funniest thing of all happened after Jade and I left school and began working in a local cafe. We both had a couple of tattoos by then, but we were keen to get matching ones. The only thing stopping us was agreeing on a design.

There were a lot of Arabic guys hanging around the cafe and both of us liked the Arabic language, the way it sounded and the way it was written. I came up with an idea that we should get a tattoo of the Arabic word for *conquer* because we were going to *conquer the world*.

The problem was that there isn't really such a word in Arabic, although one of the guys wrote down what he thought we meant. We decided it was good enough and we'd have it tattooed on the back of our legs near the ankle, out of sight but in our hearts.

The day after we got the tattoos we asked another of the guys at the cafe what he thought. The guy shook his head; it didn't mean conquer, more like that we were sad, or even mad.

'What? No way,' Jade protested. 'That's not what it means. Your mate drew it for us.' The guy just shrugged his shoulders.

We could only see the funny side of it. Whatever it actually says, the tattoo will always mean conquer to us.

CHAPTER FOUR

'This Will Be Me'

Among the files of paperwork, photographs, newspaper clippings and certificates which track my football development, there is a document titled *Katrina's sports resume*. Until researching for the book, I didn't know it existed. I think my stepmum, Michelle, must have typed it up at some stage, creating a timeline from my earliest days at Mansfield Eagles when I was chosen, aged ten, in the Redbank Plains honorary Queensland team, through all the regional, state and national teams for which I was selected and into the early years in what was then the W-League.

It's funny looking back on my achievements after all these years, and it gives me a buzz to see the road map and the journey I made. You tend to look at the big stuff when you think of your career but it's the little things that really count.

When printed out, they take up three A4-sized sheets of paper. I made my first representative team when I was selected in the Metropolitan East side in 2003. The next year I was in the Queensland under-12s. My national representation began in 2007 when I travelled with junior teams to the United Kingdom, Japan and Korea. In 2011 I was selected in the Young Matildas team, although I was injured and didn't play.

Like any career, there have been stumbles along the way, the most notable in 2007 when I was invited to join the Queensland Academy of Sport on a full contract. It was an exciting offer, given that most of the Matildas were involved with the QAS at the time, but it was soon clear that I had been thrown into an environment that intimidated rather than inspired me. I was used to challenges and pitting myself against bigger and better players but the atmosphere and expectation made me question my enjoyment of the game and, in the end, I became so conflicted that I faked injuries and illness to get out of training.

It was only a matter of time before the academy realised what was happening. Mum and Dad were called into a meeting with the senior coach, who had decided that I wasn't ready. I belonged there for my skills, he admitted, but my application was lacking. I needed to go back to playing club football with Mt Gravatt to improve my attitude and make up my mind about what I wanted. Was I serious about a football career, or not?

It was a harsh judgement in many ways and they might have focused, instead, on whether their management skills were too one-size-fits-all. Why would they believe that a fourteen-year-old could be as mature as an eighteen-year-old or a 25-year-old, who were among my training colleagues?

Dad was furious and admitted later that things had become a bit heated in the meeting. He couldn't abide someone suggesting that I was lazy. In his eyes, I was driven and the coaches should have considered my age, softened their attitude and managed me better. The journey home that evening was full of tears.

Until that moment I had only seen football as a place of joy and challenge. The future was too far away to really consider seriously, but the academy was exactly that—a serious business.

As a teenager, I had different pressures and questions as I was struggling to know and understand who I was and how to be me. I had known for years that I was gay but until then it hadn't really meant much other than I wasn't interested in boys. I was now at an age when my friends and I were starting to express ourselves socially, young adults wanting to party and rebel, and I was caught between two, competing lifestyles. Did I want to enjoy that or focus on football? There was a choice to be made.

My tears would soon dry and my disappointment turned into an important moment for me because it made me realise that I really did want a career in the game. An opportunity had suddenly been taken away and I wanted it back. Desperately. I decided that nothing was going to stop me.

As it happened, the Matildas made history later that year by reaching the quarter-finals of the Women's World Cup, winning their first game by beating Ghana 4–1—the team's first World Cup victory—and then drawing against both Norway (1–1) and Canada (2–2) to reach the knockout rounds before losing 3–2 to Brazil in a tight quarter-final.

It was an amazing achievement, particularly given there wasn't a professional competition in Australia for women, something that then head coach Tom Sermanni bemoaned after the tournament, calling it vital for the development of the game in Australia.

It was the moment that the W-League was created, and a career pathway appeared before my eyes. After the 2007 World Cup there was a promotional poster published in a newspaper of the Matildas celebrating their achievement. I cut it out and stuck it on the fridge. At the top, I scrawled: *This will be me.*

My dad, Peter, is a pretty laid-back character. He's driven trucks for most of his working life and the 900-kilometre trip down to Sydney from Brisbane is a bit like a casual Sunday drive for him. 'I enjoy a drive,' he says when I ask him. 'And Michelle doesn't mind coming along either.'

So I didn't really question it when he and Michelle began following my matches around the country, first when I was playing in junior teams and then in my early years playing in the W-League with Melbourne Victory and Adelaide United.

The first time they travelled was in 2007 when I had made the Australian schoolgirls team and we played against New Zealand in a match down in Sydney. Dad and Michelle decided on the spur of the moment to drive down and watch. They put four of the boys—Lachlan, Eden, Jared and Dylan—in the back of the eight-seater Mitsubishi Pajero and drove as far as Coffs Harbour where they stayed overnight before heading down to Sydney for the game. Members of Michelle's family who lived in Sydney were also there. The Gorry family dominated the supporters' ranks that day.

Two years later, they did the same thing, although this time the trip was twice as long because they drove to Melbourne—yes, 2000 kilometres from Brisbane to Melbourne—to watch my first game in the W-League for the Melbourne Victory.

I had signed on at Melbourne at the suggestion of Jeff Hopkins, who was in charge at QAS when I returned for a second stint in 2008, and also coached the Brisbane Roar in the first season of the new W-League. There was no room for me at Brisbane, which had a very experienced line-up, So Jeff suggested I went elsewhere to gain experience and Melbourne were interested.

In my first game, we played against Perth Glory at what was then Etihad Stadium (now Marvel). It can hold more than 53,000 people—usually AFL matches—so it was a canyon of echoes that October afternoon, as fewer than 1000 people came to watch our match, which was a double-header with the men's match being held in the evening.

It seems so long ago, and so much has changed, for me and for the sport. That night I was wearing number 13 and started on the bench, coming onto the ground in the seventy-sixth minute as we cruised to a 2–0 win to begin our season. Our current Matildas vice-captain Steph Catley was also making her debut that night, aged just fifteen, while my future Matildas team-mates Sam Kerr and Lisa De Vanna were playing for Glory.

As I ran on, I heard a piercing whistle. It was Dad, letting me know that he was in the crowd.

We call it the 'Gorry Call', with two fingers between your teeth. Dad perfected it so he could control nine kids on holidays, a skill he insisted that we all learned so we could call back to him to signal that all was well.

After the match, Dad drove twenty-three hours straight to get home, stopping occasionally for a nap on the side of the road or a quick meal at a service station or a country town. Michelle swore she would never go on another trip with him, but of course she did, on one occasion driving to Canberra for a game before continuing down to Melbourne for a second match a few days later and then driving back up to Brisbane.

The Glory match was a significant moment for me, my first match as a 'professional' footballer. I say that simply because the contract I signed paid nothing, so I was professional in the sense that I was playing the game as a career choice rather than for fitness and fun. I was not alone as most of the players held down part-time jobs, mostly menial work behind bars and reception desks, supermarkets and even gardening—jobs that were flexible enough to give us the time to train and play.

I remained at home in Brisbane and flew each week to Melbourne for home games or to join team-mates at away games. In between I trained alone, or with Brisbane Roar players, and went to work at the cafe with Jade. Mum and David footed the travel and accommodation bill.

To my delight, I recently found some archival footage of our third match that season, against Adelaide United at Hindmarsh Stadium (now Coopers), which captured my first-ever goal, a shot from twenty-five metres out which skidded past the Adelaide goalkeeper and into the net.

I had found my rhythm and confidence and, as the match wore on, made some neat passes before just missing a second goal from distance. An ABC television commentator, editing the footage for a news report, remarked: 'Katrina Gorry was in shooting mode and with a right foot like hers, why not.'

I was interviewed after the match, a fresh-faced kid with tousled hair and a big grin on my face, enveloped in a rush of goodwill after my goal. 'I didn't think about it. I turned around and my team-mates shouted, "You scored!" and we all celebrated. It was great.'

I scored again a few matches later and even though the team failed to make the finals, fading to finish fifth after a promising start, the team disappointment was offset by my rapid improvement as a player, topped off by being named as the club's young player of the year.

It was an exciting beginning to the career I desperately wanted, but I felt like I needed more playing time so I opted to leave Melbourne Victory and join Adelaide United for the 2010 season, again unpaid but with a promise of being in the starting line-up. I had to dip into my savings from my cafe job and the Bank of Mum helped out as I decided to live in Adelaide, away from home, as part of the experience. A couple of my Brisbane friends had also joined the team, so it was a fun year off the field but a strange and humbling experience on it as we were beaten in every game and finished a distant last.

So it was back to Melbourne in 2011. The club understood why I had gone to Adelaide and welcomed me back, even agreeing to pay me $100 per match, my first wages as a footballer!

My best performance, at least in terms of goal-scoring, came in December when we travelled across the continent to Perth to play the Glory and walked away 5–0 winners. I scored a brace that day, although it was our captain Jodie Taylor who took the headlines with a hat-trick.

We managed to squeeze our way into the finals but it would be a brief experience, knocked over by Canberra because of a late goal by their star striker, Michelle Heyman. It was my first gutting experience as a player as we were denied a place in our first grand final.

I'd met Michelle a few times. She was an imposing figure on the field but a happy, friendly person socially. I had no idea how important she would be to me later, after we became Matildas team-mates.

CHAPTER FIVE
A Dream Fulfilled

I am a good sleeper on aeroplanes. Perhaps it's an advantage of being small, but I usually nod off soon after the plane takes off and levels out. Somehow I'm able to ignore the engine noise and discomfort of upright seats.

I was grateful for this skill in March 2012 when I ventured out into the world—both to test myself as a player and as a young woman experiencing life away from my family for the first time.

I had landed a contract to play a northern hemisphere summer season in Canada with the semi-professional Ottawa Fury. They were based in the country's capital city and competed in the second-tier North American league.

The Fury already had a history of taking young Australian players—a dozen or so over the past six seasons—so it wasn't difficult to arrange an offer to play there after my second season with Melbourne Victory. My pay would barely cover the living costs of the three-month stint, but it seemed worth the plunge in terms of my development as a player.

But the closer it came to my departure, the more anxious I became about my decision. I could easily have stayed home and had six months off between seasons, resting my body and working on my ball skills, but the world was calling and if I wanted a proper career as a footballer then it had to start sometime and somewhere. So why not now and in Canada? After all, their national team consistently ranked above Australia in the FIFA world rankings.

I might seem tough and even aggressive at times on the pitch, but inside I can be a bit of a softy, and my send-off at Brisbane Airport with Mum and Dad and my stepmum was a sob-fest. To makes matters worse, there were two stopovers on the way to Canada, which only raised my anxiety levels about missing connecting flights and whether I was doing the right thing. That's why I was so grateful for my habit of sleeping on the plane.

Even so, the fourteen-hour time difference ensured I was pretty jetlagged by the time I arrived in Ottawa. I wandered through the baggage area to collect my things and then headed for the exit where I had arranged to meet the coach, Dominic Oliveri. Then it dawned on me that I had no idea what he looked like.

The arrivals area was teeming with people. I scanned the crowd, hoping Dominic would spot me and introduce himself. I finally saw a man dressed in a black tracksuit with the club's fire badge embroidered on the front.

He smiled when he saw me walking towards him. 'It's always easy to spot the smaller ones,' he said and laughed. I wasn't offended, just relieved.

The team's headquarters were in MacLaren Street, which cuts through the city centre, and the players were housed in various flats along nearby streets. I was rooming with three American girls. When I arrived there was a team party already underway, a sort of get-together as the season was just a couple of weeks away. All my fears disappeared when I realised that I had found myself a new family.

Being focused entirely on the job of being a footballer, living and breathing the game—eat, sleep, play, train and repeat—was a surreal experience. We trained in the evenings under lights, starting at 9 pm after the men's team had finished, which meant we didn't get home until after 11 pm. It was strange for an Aussie girl like me, who was used to getting up with the sunrise, and I often found myself walking through town, alone, in the early mornings waiting for the cafes to open while my team-mates slept.

Our flat was next door to a homeless shelter. We could see the residents from our back door, sitting out the back smoking and talking—men and women of all ages who had had it tough and needed a hand to survive. We introduced ourselves and started listening to their stories, usually in the afternoons before we went to training. Many of them had drug problems and stories of abuse or neglect. The faces changed frequently so there was never enough time to establish friendships but it was a rewarding, fleeting experience that I would later come to appreciate even more when drug abuse affected my family.

The club gave us food vouchers, usually to pizza restaurants in the city, and we often gave our unused ones to our neighbours. As the season came to a close, and summer turned to autumn, we sent over a heap of clothes, like tracksuits that we didn't need anymore that could be useful to them. None of us was earning much money but it felt good to give back when we could.

I was at training one evening when the coach, Dom, called me over. 'Have you heard the news? You've been called up into the squad for the Australian team.'

I stood there, stunned. No, I hadn't heard the news. Back in Australia, Mum was the point of contact for things like this but she had missed the email. I walked back towards my team-mates with a silly grin on my face, but also telling myself that it was just the squad and I shouldn't get my hopes up. Still, it was a big moment for me and I rang Mum. She found the email and we both squealed with delight.

Two days later Dom called me over again as we readied for training. 'I've been told that I have to give you the next two weeks off,' he began with a scowl on his face. I was puzzled until Dom grinned. 'You've made the team,' he said, 'you're flying to Tokyo to play against Japan.'

This time I couldn't contain myself and I ran back to my team-mates, who all screamed and leaped in the air as we hugged. It was as if we had scored a goal to win the World Cup.

I rang Mum. 'Right, I'm coming over. I want to be there,' she declared.

I didn't expect to play much, if at all, and I was nervous considering we were playing the best team in the world at the time. So I spoke to Tameka Butt (now Yallop) to get some advice. She had been a Matilda since 2007 and was playing club football in America at the time. Tameka agreed with me about playing against Japan. 'They're like chasing shadows,' she told me. 'If you get on the pitch just make sure you enjoy the experience.'

I was on a plane a few days later and arrived to find my new team-mates in a camp in the outer suburbs of Tokyo. I knew most of them—the team was largely made up of Queenslanders at the time—so it helped ease my nerves and allowed me to concentrate on the game ahead.

There were 20,000 people in Japan's National Stadium on the afternoon of 11 July 2012. The atmosphere was amazing, particularly given that this was a friendly, with no consequences for either side.

Japan were the reigning world champions and on their way to the London Olympics. By contrast, the Matildas were ranked eleventh in the world and we'd been knocked out of the World Cup in the quarter-finals the year before. The team had also missed an Olympics berth after finishing behind Japan and North Korea in qualifying. It was a time of rebuilding and looking to the future.

My moment had arrived, and I welled up in tears as the two teams stood for their national anthems. So did Mum, who I could see in the crowd. It's almost impossible to put into words just how emotional a moment like that is to a sportsperson who has dreamed and been driven by this potential moment all their lives. You imagine sometimes what it will feel like but when the moment actually arrives it is almost overwhelming.

Predictably, we were completely outclassed in the game, losing 3–0 to a team that would go on to win Olympic silver a month later. A penalty in the twenty-fifth minute and a tap-in from a right-wing cross ensured the match was safe for the home side by half-time. We improved in the second half, but Japan still added a third goal before we had a rare shot on goal that might have given us some respectability.

I watched all this from the benches, hoping I would get some game time in front of the biggest crowd I had seen at a women's match. I got my chance in the sixty-fifth minute, replacing Alanna Kennedy. I sprinted out onto the ground as if my life depended on it. I spent the next thirty minutes running around after the Japanese shadows, just as Tameka had described. I think I only touched the ball a couple of times but it didn't dampen my emotions or my pride. It was one of the best nights of my life.

After the game I made my way up the stands to see Mum. I had to walk past hundreds of Japanese fans who wanted to high-five me. They were the best crowd—football lovers who were just pleased to see us compete. They applauded as Mum and I hugged and cried in the stands. My dream had come true.

Coach Tom Sermanni's post-match comments also gave me some heart. Yes, he conceded, the Matildas were outclassed, but there was hope: 'It was a good chance for some of our younger players to see competition at this level and we've got to remember that we've given debuts to six players in our past three matches. We're at the very start of a rebuilding phase but I think we've got some great talent coming through.'

If I kept my focus and put in the hard work, then I could be part of the Matildas' future. Back in Brisbane, the Matildas poster with my scrawled vow on top was still on the fridge.

Mum and I barely had time for a celebratory meal before I was on my way back to Ottawa to rejoin my Fury teammates and attend to unfinished business. The season had been spectacular for the club. In the past, the Fury had frequently won its division title in Canada only to fall short at the national finals.

During the twelve-week regular season we had won ten and lost two matches, finishing on top of the Central Division and advancing to the nationals where we were due to meet Washington United, who were favoured to win even though we had the home field advantage.

Personally, I'd had a really good season. Coach Dom had encouraged me to take an on-field leadership role and control the games from midfield. I felt comfortable and encouraged to develop that role as an architect, if I can call it that. My team-mates and I were all around the same age with the same desire to improve and we were very supportive of one another.

A decent crowd of over 600 were there to see us score just before half-time and then hang on in the second half for a 1–0 win. It was a hard-fought victory in a game with plenty of emotion, particularly in the second half as Washington tried to equalise. My passion got the better of me as the game grew tenser and earned me a yellow card, which I had to manage carefully in the last, desperate minutes. The final whistle was a relief.

Our opponents in the final were the Pali Blues from Los Angeles, the clear favourites and defending champions who had been victorious in all but one of their fourteen regular season games and had comfortably won their semi-final.

And for ninety-two minutes of the game in Ottawa, watched by more than 1000 people, it looked as if they would beat us. They'd scored in the first two minutes of the game and then held off everything we'd thrown at them in the second half. Towards the end of injury time we got a free kick deep in their territory. It was our last chance.

I took the kick and struck it well. Their goalkeeper could only parry the ball away and our striker Ashley Seal pounced on the loose ball and buried it into the net. Equaliser! We had seized the psychological advantage. Six minutes into extra time I found myself thirty metres out and in the clear. I love the opportunity to let fly from thirty metres and watch the ball dip and swerve into the corner of the goal. It was one of my trademarks, but this time my shot rattled off the crossbar.

We were still tied after thirty minutes of extra time and had to go to penalties. Our captain and goalkeeper, Jasmine Phillips, came up with two inspiring saves to give our team a 5–4 victory. Thankfully, I didn't have to take a penalty. I hate them because they are such a brutal end to a game. More on that later.

It was my first club title and the first for the Fury, so the feeling of euphoria was exhilarating, particularly when I was named in the league's all-star team. I had tasted a championship and I wanted more.

I headed back to Australia, sad to leave but eager to join Brisbane Roar.

CHAPTER SIX

A Roaring Success

'Brisbane local Katrina Gorry will play for her hometown club after two seasons with Melbourne Victory.'

The announcement on Brisbane Roar's website by Belinda Wilson, the team's new head coach, was about as low key as you could get amid the excitement of the club's other recruitments for the 2012–13 season, which suited me fine.

I had made my debut for the Matildas in Tokyo and had appeared in a couple of friendlies since, but the truth was that I was still very much a young, up-and-coming player, just turned twenty years old with much to learn. And I desperately wanted to play for my hometown team.

I'd had to go away to gain experience, and had now returned after my stints with Melbourne Victory, Adelaide United and Ottawa Fury, having developed as a player and as a person. This was the first opportunity I'd had to wriggle my way into a team that was used to success, so I took it with both hands.

I was friends with a lot of the Brisbane girls and I knew about Belinda's coaching experience so I arranged a conversation with her soon after she was appointed. She said she liked the way I played and that was that. Deal done.

We were a formidable team on paper, with a number of national team players including our then captain Clare Polkinghorne, as well as Elise Kellond-Knight, Tameka Butt, Amy Chapman, Brooke Spence and Laura Alleway (now Brock) who were regular players. Emily Gielnik, who had made her national team debut alongside me in Tokyo, was also on the roster.

After a flat performance in a 0–0 draw with Canberra in the opening game in late October and a couple of losses in November, we hit our straps through December and January to win the regular season premiership with eight wins from twelve matches.

On a personal level I enjoyed a pretty decent season and although I had only scored twice, both were important contributions. The first came late in the home game against Perth Glory in round eight. Perth had held a 2–0 lead well into the second half before Tameka gave us some hope when she scored after a shot by Emily was blocked. As the minutes ticked down, Tameka set me up at the top of the box and I let fly with a drive that rattled into the right-hand corner of the net, levelling scores in a game we felt we had stolen from Perth. Ultimately, it was the difference in staying ahead of them in the title race.

My second goal came when we hosted Canberra in the last game of the season which we needed to win to lift the silverware for the minor premiership. This time there would be no nerves as we began with an intent to win well. We had chances in the opening minutes and then I got away down the left wing. Once I was alongside the box, I cut back and hit a low, teasing cross as Tameka made a run. She missed, but so did the Canberra goalkeeper as my ball found the far side netting. From then on the match was never in doubt as we ran out 5–1 winners.

The excitement of winning that title was dulled somewhat when, in the post season competition, we lost our semi-final 3–2 to Sydney, thanks to a Sam Kerr double. Sydney had finished fourth in the regular season but went on to win the grand final 3–1 against Melbourne Victory.

Not everything is measured by goals, of course. In many ways, the number of assists I had made were a much better way of judging my impact as a midfielder. Tameka and I combined really well on the field that season, and she was the second highest goal-scorer in the league. Scoring two goals myself was a bonus.

I even won a couple of media awards and was included in a team of the year as the best attacking midfielder in the W-League. It was pretty heady stuff for a 21-year-old, particularly as the season would be regarded as the most productive ever for the emergence of local talent, later labelled as the Matildas' 'golden generation'.

Apart from myself and Emily Gielnik, there was Sam Kerr, Kyah Simon, Caitlin Foord, Alanna Kennedy and Steph Catley, who would all help form the nucleus of the national team for the next decade, and who were such an important component in our success at the 2023 World Cup.

I had played three more games for the Matildas by the end of 2012, tasting a mix of success and failure and seeing off my first coach—Tom Sermanni—before I'd really got to know him.

In November we had travelled to Shenzhen, in China, to participate in a qualifying tournament for the East Asian Football Federation Cup. It was the first (and last) time that Australia was invited, and we had to win the five-day round-robin event against Chinese Taipei (Taiwan), Hong Kong and hosts China to qualify for the tournament proper against Japan and North and South Korea, which would be played in July 2013.

I came on as a substitute against Chinese Taipei and, rather satisfyingly, had a hand in the last goal of the 7–0 rout. Then, two nights later, I started against Hong Kong and recorded an assist in the first of four unanswered goals. It was an emphatic victory which put us firmly on the path towards qualification.

Tom was swinging the changes to give a lot of the younger members of the squad a chance to shine so I was back on the bench for the final match against China which we only had to draw to qualify. Sadly we lost 2–1 against a much more experienced team. It would prove to be Tom's last game in charge as he was scouted to coach the USA women's team, the number one team in FIFA's world rankings, an appointment he could not have resisted.

—

A few days before Christmas 2012, Hesterine de Reus was appointed to replace Tom, and she faced an uphill battle before she'd even arrived. Some of the girls had sent off a letter to Football Federation Australia (FFA) expressing concerns that they would appoint a female coach simply because it looked good to appoint a woman, particularly as the Matildas had always been coached by a man. The players thought this was a bad decision and tokenism at its worst. The new coach should be the best person for the job, not the best political choice.

When we found out that Hesterine had applied for the job there was concern from some of the girls that she was not a good fit, culturally at least. Tom was a very laid-back character and we had even enjoyed personal freedom (to a point) under his leadership when in training camps. We might have been young adults but as elite sportspeople we already lived very responsible and dedicated lifestyles and didn't need to be corralled by officialdom.

Our fear was that Hesterine was from a very different, very structured culture with the Dutch style of football management. Those fears were quickly realised when we came together for a camp at the end of the 2012–13 domestic season. Hesterine, who had watched all the W-League finals and named a large squad, was insistent that the team should be 'more professional' in its approach, and she even disliked players taking contracts with overseas clubs in the off-season.

We quickly learned that there were new rules to be obeyed when in camp. We had strict schedules that including having to all dress in the same uniform, having set 'nap' times between training sessions, common rooms cleared by 10 pm and very little real free time where we could go outside the camp.

Hesterine even tried to control what we ate. She would make comments, like telling some girls they 'shouldn't be eating that' which caused some real problems later on. I know that Michelle Heyman went through a particularly tough time. We had to weigh in and weigh out every day and there were times that I could hear players discussing not eating meals because their weight had fluctuated by a few grams. It made no sense and did not take into account that we might be on our periods.

I was reluctant to cast judgement—that's not my way—and, anyway, I was a young player and eager just to be in the team. If someone wanted to tell me what to wear then I was happy because it meant that I didn't have to think about it.

Equally, I loved napping after training so I was hardly going to complain when I was told to go to bed and rest.

It would be six months before Hesterine got to manage a Matildas match—two friendlies against New Zealand in the middle of a bitter Canberra winter. It was hardly the ideal beginning for her or the team as we struggled to maintain match fitness after the end of the domestic season. Such was the low-key nature of the New Zealand matches that the first was held behind closed doors at the Australian Institute of Sport. The second match was at McKellar Park in front of a small crowd for a trophy called the Centenary Cup, which we ended up winning when a penalty shootout was required after a 1–1 draw.

A few weeks later we jetted off to Holland for what was called a European tour. It was, in fact, two matches in a week, the first against the Netherlands and the other in Paris a week later against France, rated fourth in the FIFA rankings at that time compared to our ninth place. Both sides were at full strength and gearing up for the European championships.

The matches against the Netherlands and France were both special for me. Our team had travelled across the world and were not match fit so we expected little other than a spirited effort against two highly ranked teams.

I was a late inclusion in the starting line-up because of a training injury sustained by Servet Uzunlar. This was my big opportunity. The team started well and had some early chances that went begging. I was combining well with

Emily van Egmond to control the midfield and force the Dutch to go long, so it was against the run of play when they scored midway through the half to set us back on our heels.

But we persisted and, not long afterwards, I found myself free just outside the box. I hit a left-foot volley that thudded into the net. A wonder strike, they called it later. The truth was that it was on my wrong side, so I was just trying to ensure that I didn't miss the ball completely.

It was a moment that I won't forget—my first goal in the green and gold—even if it was in front of a few hundred people in a faraway town. I ran around the park like a headless chook in celebration.

The teams were level at half-time but our lack of match fitness was evident in the second half as the Netherlands scored twice more for a comfortable 3–1 victory. Hesterine was impressed with our first half but thought we'd fallen away in the second.

She was less impressed three days later when we lost 1–0 to a second-string Dutch club side, ADO Den Haag, who we played in the city of Delft on our way to France. To make matters worse, they scored on a counter-attack after a Matildas' corner was cleared away, leaving a lone defender. Hesterine did not mince words: 'I am disappointed in losing to a club side. I think it should be impossible. We cannot let it happen again.'

We didn't, and surprised many when we beat the highly fancied French side, which had finished fourth at both the last World Cup and Olympics Games. France looked the better side for much of the game and it was only our resolute defence that kept us in the game until Tameka Butt scored with a brilliant volley from a set-piece.

I started on the bench but came on after half-time and got involved at both ends of the pitch, clearing the ball off the line to save a goal and then, in the seventieth minute, the ball fell my way a good thirty metres from goal. I could see that the goalkeeper had advanced off her line. 'What the heck,' I thought, 'I'll give it a shot.' I struck the shot well, this time with my right foot and watched in what seemed like slow motion as the ball headed towards the top right-hand corner of the net. The keeper was beaten but I sensed that she thought it was going to go high; instead it dipped and nestled in the back of the net—my second goal in as many matches settled a fantastic 2–0 win.

The Emily Morgan Hotel in San Antonio, Texas, is billed as the most haunted hotel in America. It is an imposing Gothic-inspired structure, a former medical facility complete with a morgue and decorated with gargoyles that portray various medical ailments before it was converted into a hotel in the mid-1970s.

The hotel also overlooks the Alamo Mission, site of the famous nineteenth-century battle in which 600 men were killed, including famed frontiersman Davy Crockett. The hotel is named after a servant girl whose role in the subsequent Battle of San Jacinto inspired the song 'The Yellow Rose of Texas'.

The reason I tell this story is because the Matildas stayed in the Emily Morgan for a week during October 2013 during a five-day training camp and one-off match against the USA.

It seemed a strange trip to make—an eighteen-hour flight across the Pacific for one match and a camp that could have taken place in Brisbane—but in hindsight it was worth it just for the experience of the Emily Morgan.

I don't believe in ghosts, or at least I didn't until we stayed there.

It was Halloween while we were there and when we went out to explore the city one night there were clowns everywhere. That seems innocent enough except that one of our players—I won't say who—is scared of clowns. Her fear was obvious and one of the clowns in the street couldn't help himself and chased her all the way back to the hotel.

In the early hours of the morning there was some seriously weird stuff going on. Sam Kerr woke up around 3 am and swore that she saw people moving about in her room. Other girls reported that the door handle of their room rattled, as if someone was trying to get in, and bathroom taps were turned on.

The reception desk bell would ding mysteriously and we were told that the hotel CCTV had captured images of 'orbs', like bright shining lights, around the corridors. Not to mention doors closing for no reason, elevators stopping suddenly, the sound of a hospital cart being wheeled down a corridor and strange, antiseptic smells.

As far as the match was concerned, we lost 4–0, which was unsurprising given their strength at the time and how little we had played during the year under Hesterine, who was not impressed by that result, as you might expect. Her assessment was blunt: 'The defending part of our game was not good enough. Conceding four goals was way too much.'

We returned to Australia where we had two more international matches, both against China, which were important pointers for our defence of the Asian Cup, which was to be played in mid-2014.

Although I had played in the matches against New Zealand earlier in the year, these two matches felt as if they were the first chance I'd had to play as a Matilda in front of a home crowd, the first at Wollongong on 24 November.

I was on a golden run as I again found myself in the thick of things, having a shot blocked in the thirty-fourth minute before regathering the ball, forcing myself past two defenders and thrashing a left-foot shot into the roof of the net. My third goal in four matches. I had a hand in our second goal a few minutes later and had two more shots in the second half, buoyed by Hesterine's encouragement to shoot when I got the chance.

'I don't think I've scored so many goals in my life,' I beamed in a television interview afterwards, still flushed from the game. I was asked what had changed in the team since Hesterine's arrival, and my answers hinted at the controversy that was to come. We were more disciplined, we went to team meetings and had naps. 'There's no dawdling, just get things done and focus on football.'

We completed a clean sweep at Parramatta three days later, establishing a two-goal lead in the first half before China got a goal late in the game through a penalty. I didn't score but provided the centring ball that resulted in our first goal. It was a satisfying end to the year but the coach was far from happy. 'We didn't play well but we won,' Hesterine said. 'I thought we had some poor defending and poor passing but winning is a positive.'

Behind the scenes there was growing resentment about Hesterine, not only about her management but also the style of play she was instilling in us. Gone was our natural aggression and the pressure we liked to apply to the opposition; instead, we had established a quite defensive 4–3–3 formation.

I was trapped, in a way. Hesterine had a lot of belief in me and a player can't ask for much more than that from a coach. She was very encouraging to me personally at a time when everything I touched seemed to turn to gold. Even so,

I could see the mood of the player group and it was clear that there was a significant problem as other players were not enjoying their time in camp. The next year was not going to be easy.

CHAPTER SEVEN

'She's Done It Again'

My abiding memory of Hesterine de Reus is a McDonald's meal smuggled into a hotel in the Cypriot town of Larnaca in the European spring of 2014.

Hesterine had already established herself as a guard dog when it came to most things, especially food. As far as she was concerned, there was no excuse for poor food choices, even after a match when most of the girls liked to get a burger and chips because we had expended vast amounts of energy and were in a recovery phase.

So when we arrived on the island in March 2014 for the Cyprus Cup, we had a problem. The entire place seemed to shut down during the mid-afternoon and we were all starving. We checked into our hotel and some of the girls decided to head into the town to see what we could get to eat.

Macca's seemed the only choice so we decided as a group to risk Hesterine's wrath and sneak back into the rooms with bags full of hamburgers and fries, then shovel it into our mouths quickly in case Hesterine suddenly turned up. She didn't, and we ate our fill, but there were far more serious problems for us than secret junk food.

We were effectively in lockdown in the hotel, refused permission to leave even to meet our parents who had travelled across the world. If Hesterine thought the tactic would improve team morale and bonding then she was as misguided about that as she was about nutrition. It would be the straw that broke the camel's back.

The strange thing about the Cyprus Cup is that the host nation has never competed, instead inviting a dozen teams who are divided into three groups and play off in a round-robin style.

We were in Group B, drawn with France, Scotland and the Netherlands, and needing to win at least two of the games to ensure that we could play off in the final.

Things got off to a bad start, 2–0 down at half-time to the Dutch. Michelle Heyman and I had both started the match on the bench and came on in the second half as the team began to lift.

My form continued to shine as I took a pass from Steph Catley and scored a nice goal while Michelle chipped the Dutch keeper five minutes later to bring us level. I had a chance to score the winner soon after but missed and we settled for the comeback draw.

We faced France, ranked fifth in the world then, two days later in the nearby city of Nicosia. Again, we began slowly as the French scored three times in the first half to all but put the game out of reach. We again lifted in the second half and scored twice, the first through Sam Kerr and then Emily van Egmond, who slotted home a penalty, but that's as close as we got.

A win against Scotland had become a necessity but, yet again, we started poorly and fell 3–0 behind before Michelle scored twice to give us faint hope. Instead, it was Scotland who scored again for a solid 4–2 win.

It put us in a playoff for seventh place against Italy as we finally got some rhythm and scored five times, including another goal from me, before Italy scored two late consolation goals in the last five minutes. It was a long way short of Hesterine's expectations as we headed back to Australia.

We had two more matches before the Asian Cup, both against Brazil and played in my hometown, but trouble was brewing off the field as players had finally had enough of Hesterine's ways and complained to the FFA via the players' federation.

The story of the players' mutiny broke in the days before the first match against Brazil, forcing Hesterine to go public and insist that she had not lost control of the team and that there was no crisis, just a small group of disgruntled players. We lost the first match 1–0, which was a decent performance in the circumstances. Although Hesterine was videoed giving high fives to players on the bench, the mood inside the change rooms was now pretty grim.

Even though we came out three days later and beat Brazil 2–1, it was pretty clear that the FFA would have little choice but to let Hesterine go. A week later she was gone and Alen Stajcic, the Sydney Football Club coach, was installed as interim coach to take us to the Asian Cup and, hopefully, the 2015 World Cup in Canada.

—

Our plans were now in turmoil, caught between two coaches and two playing styles with less than a month before the Asian Cup in Vietnam, the most important tournament in our recent history. We were the defending champions, having beaten North Korea in the 2010 final, but for the most part, we had struggled in a tournament that had been around since 1975.

Far from being settled and playing well, 'Staj', as we knew him, wanted the team to revert to its hallmark aggressive playing style and drop the defensive, possession strategies demanded by Hesterine.

The task could not be understated because we were facing teams like Japan, China and North and South Korea, although it had been eased somewhat because of a decision by FIFA to expand the World Cup tournament from sixteen to twenty-four teams, meaning that five Asian teams would be invited to Brazil.

Ho Chi Minh City is a bubbling hive of humanity, defined by its rivers and canals, and though most of us had just come from our own Australian summer season and were used to hot conditions, Vietnam was a different level weather-wise. The wet season had just begun and temperatures were now northward of thirty degrees, coupled with humidity of more than eighty per cent. Even the grass was different and a bit sticky. 'Steamy' would be a polite description as we faced the prospect of five matches in less than two weeks.

Other than a corked thigh, I was feeling fantastic. The goals had kept coming for me as well as my room-mate Michelle Heyman. Not only did we have an almost instant connection and friendship off the field, but it seemed to be matched by an innate, on-field understanding. We knew where each other was on the pitch and which one of us would make a run. With Sam Kerr coming back after an injury, it would be up to us to lead the team forward.

I was an unusual attacking midfielder in that I liked working hard, not just forward and taking the occasional shot at goal but also defensively. I liked being a workhorse but it was across the top of the box that I was receiving the most encouragement. It was a simple equation. The more opportunities I got to shoot, the more I tried and the more I scored.

Our first match was our most important test, against Japan on a hot evening at Thong Nhat Stadium. Midway through the second half we held a 2–0 lead thanks to a fantastic goal from Caitlin Foord, who ran from halfway and beat a couple of defenders before scoring off the inside of the post.

Lisa De Vanna, who had been denied in the opening minutes, then extended our lead against the run of play. Japan had had their own chances, kept out by our goalkeeper Lydia Williams, before their captain Aya Miyama, whom I was guarding, got away and rattled the crossbar.

It was new territory for us against Japan, rare to be dominant on the scorecard against a side we normally feared so much that we changed our attacking style to play man-on-man containment because of their passing skills.

As the inevitable pressure built in the second half we dropped our guard and Japan scored, first through a defensive error which ended in an own goal and then, with just six minutes to go and after some hectic end-to-end action, when substitute Yuki Ogimi (now Nagasato) got through the defence and netted from close range.

It was hard not to be disappointed with a draw after conceding a 2–0 lead, but Staj saw the positive side, as he told the media: 'The first thirty minutes were really good, which we dominated, and we can take a lot from that. I thought we looked comfortable at half-time but then they came out and played like one of the best teams in the world.

There was some great defending from us, and I'm happy to get a point. We will improve every game from here.'

Our second match, against Jordan, was just two days later and Staj decided it was a good opportunity to rotate the squad, particularly given the trying conditions. It was a game we expected to win well but nothing should be taken for granted in an international.

Staj wasn't joking, making ten changes which set us back in the first half as we struggled for fluency until Kate Gill, filling in as captain, struck twice either side of half-time to become the Matildas' greatest goal-scorer at the time.

I sat on the bench until the sixty-sixth minute and then came on eager to make a difference. I was never a great bench player, although under Hesterine I had only started on the bench to give me a rest if we were playing an easy game or as a super-sub if she needed to inject me into the game.

That's exactly what I was just minutes after coming onto the ground, receiving a pass from Sam Kerr on the left wing and dribbling into the box. I could have passed it but saw the goalkeeper had left an opening so I hit it with the outside of my foot and watched it curve into the bottom right-hand side of the net. Bang. Goal. I was pretty pleased with the shot because it took the match beyond Jordan's reach, even though they scored late.

Our last match in the group stage was against the hosts, Vietnam, who had been beaten 4–0 by Japan. We had a heap of chances in the first half but couldn't get the ball in the net until Vietnam scored a comical own goal just before half-time.

The heavens opened in the second half, reducing the game to a scrappy affair as we worried about monsoonal conditions and lightning strikes near the ground. Right on full-time I got the ball in the middle of the ground, used my speed to get past a couple of defenders and took a flying shot from thirty-five metres into the top left-hand side of the net. Goal.

'Everyone who knows Katrina Gorry knows that once she has beaten that extra defender then she is going to take a shot,' the Fox Sports commentator observed.

The win ensured that we qualified for the World Cup in Canada while we would face South Korea four days later in the semi-final after finishing behind Japan on goal difference. We knew it would be a tough game, especially as we were all starting to feel the pinch physically because of the weather.

Everyone was telling me before the game to make sure I took shots if there was an opportunity. I was in such good form that it seemed as if every time I took a shot on goal, it either went close or went in. Sam Kerr, who was starting the game on the bench, insisted that if I scored again, I had to run over to her and 're-enact the Lion King'—leap into her arms and she would hold me up in celebration.

And that's exactly what happened. We had a bunch of chances in the first half without a result but a few minutes into the second half, Caitlin Foord recovered the ball after a goalmouth scrimmage and passed it back to me in the middle of the ground. I saw my chance, took a couple of steps and buried the ball into the top right netting. The place went into a frenzy.

'Katrina Gorry, she's done it again,' the Fox Sports commentator called as I sprinted over to Sam on the sidelines and leaped into her arms, as she'd asked, while the team around us held up their hands in celebration.

Our lead didn't last long, however, as South Korea fought back and scored through a penalty, which set up a thrilling finale. We continued to press forward as first Lisa and then Michelle came close before an angled free kick by Elise Kellond-Knight found its way through a sea of legs to score with barely ten minutes left in the game.

Japan won the other semi-final against China which set up a replay of our earlier game against the Japanese, this time in front of 10,000 spectators. We were excited by our chances because Sam Kerr was coming back into the starting line-up, and she almost scored twice in the opening minutes but missed narrowly.

Japan then settled and began to create some chances of their own. In the twenty-eighth minute they won a corner. The ball was played short and then crossed high across the face of goal where their tall forward Azusa Iwashimizu nodded it in from the back post in a well-executed corner.

Japan had the upper hand but we continued to press and the second half turned into a thrilling encounter with chances at both ends of the ground. Sam went close a couple of times, denied by an offside call, and Michelle, Lisa and Teigen Allen were also unlucky not to score.

In the end Japan held on to victory. We were all exhausted from the effort of five games in just fourteen days, but through the disappointment of missed chances Staj saw a bright side. 'I'm proud of how much the team has improved in the tournament. Hopefully by the time we reach the World Cup next year we can improve that little bit more in our execution and beat those big countries.'

My role had changed for the final game. I was again tasked with keeping quiet Japan's captain Aya Miyama, but this time without the freedom of pressing forward, as I had done in earlier matches. It was a task I found all the more difficult because of my admiration for Aya as a player. I did a decent job, I thought, and she clearly had some respect for me because we exchanged shirts after the game. As it turned out, Miyama was voted player of the tournament while I was runner-up.

CHAPTER EIGHT

A Cinderella Story

I've never been a girl who dresses up in haute couture and heels. I'd rather not wear a dress of any kind, but in November 2014 I had no choice.

It was my own fault, I suppose. I'd had a fantastic year with Brisbane and the Matildas in Vietnam. I was looking forward to a mini break before the start of the W-League season when I got a phone call telling me that I was a finalist in the Asian Player of the Year award.

Individual honours are not something I normally think about. It's the team performance that really matters to me—a premiership is the ultimate goal rather than being the best individual player. But I knew that this award was a big deal and that I would have to go to Manila for the presentation.

Mum, of course, was thrilled and immediately brought up the need for me to wear an evening gown.

'I'm not going to win,' I protested.

'That's not the point. You still have to look nice for the ceremony.'

I couldn't argue with her so we went shopping a day or so later to find a gown. I am a nightmare to go shopping with because I generally refuse to try anything on. Mum is very patient and tries her best but my instinctive response is either that the garment won't fit or will look awful.

But this was different, and Mum wasn't going to let me off as we wandered along James Street, Brisbane's upmarket shopping strip. To say that I was out of my comfort zone is an understatement. Thankfully, almost immediately there was one dress that we both liked: a black gown with a white underlay which showed off my shoulders—after all, a girl has to be strong even when she's glammed up.

We went back and forth a few times to other shops but kept coming back to the first choice. I liked it but was dubious because it was quite expensive and I thought I'd probably never wear it again. I eventually relented.

The next problem was shoes. I had a pair in my wardrobe which were bought for a school formal years before, so I didn't need to buy a new pair. But walking in them was another matter, so Mum, who can sprint in heels, spent a few hours teaching me how to walk without falling over and breaking my ankles.

Mum had every reason to be cautious about heels. Many years before, when I was quite young, we were out in the city one night and we ended up at the South Bank ferry terminal. As we crossed the footbridge near the restaurants, it began raining in a very Brisbane-like manner—suddenly and heavily.

Mum, who was in heels, was getting soaked and questioned why we weren't running to get to the car. She took off before the rest of us could say anything but only got a few metres before she went over the edge and into the water.

We all stopped and looked on in horror as she disappeared from sight. Then an arm appeared, gripping her handbag, which was placed back on the bridge, followed by the arm again, this time holding the bedraggled pair of shoes. Finally, Mum's head appeared as she clambered out, dripping wet and pissed off as we tried hard not to collapse in fits of laughter.

It was so out of character for Mum to do anything silly and she was *so* embarrassed. We still tell the story of 'Linda's Lake' at family dinners.

Mum, Dad and I flew business class (thanks to the organisers) to Manila a week or so later for the glitzy ceremony. On the flight, Mum started nagging me about preparing a speech—a task I believed was pointless since I was up against two Japanese players, Nahomi Kawasumi and Aya Miyama, who I'd marked at the Asian Cup.

Surely one of them would win, particularly as Japan had beaten us in the cup final. Miyama had won the past two awards and the Japanese team's performances over the year ensured that she would poll very well again with the judges. Being a finalist was reward enough.

'I don't need to prepare a speech because I'm not going to win,' I told Mum, 'so relax.'

Mum wasn't satisfied and kept at me after we arrived. The fact that we were picked up at the Ninoy Aquino Airport by a chauffeured limousine and taken to the Makati Shangri-La, probably the most luxurious hotel I'd ever been in, didn't help as it made Mum more convinced than ever that I had won.

I practised walking in heels up and down the corridor outside the room, keen to avoid making a fool of myself, but I still refused to sit down and plan a speech because I couldn't allow myself the hope that I could possibly win.

The hotel foyer—complete with fountain—was full of dignitaries when we went downstairs that night, and it was beginning to dawn on me that this was an important night for the game.

I had won individual awards before but they were normally presented immediately after a game or tournament when we were still sweaty in our kit and people were on their way home. But here in the hotel's massive ballroom, with its white-rose bouquets and chandeliers, there were hundreds of people sipping champagne and eating canapes brought around by carefully styled waitstaff.

During the evening there were a dozen or so awards to hand out—for fair play, young players, national and domestic teams, coaches of the year and even referees. Australians featured prominently, with Tony Popovic winning coach of the year for leading Western Sydney Wanderers to win the AFC Champions League and Crystal Palace midfielder Mile Jedinak winning the international player of the year.

My award section was the finale, along with the men's prize, which was won by Saudi Arabian star striker Nasser Al-Shamrani. I had been quite calm until then, but when FIFA president Sepp Blatter stepped forward to make the presentations, my nerves began to jangle.

Then my name was called.

'Katrina, Katrina. It's you, it's you!' Mum was shouting and shunting me out of my seat before my brain had registered that I'd actually won. I was the AFC Women's Player of the Year. It was surreal.

The music blared, the applause rang out and camera lights shone in my face as I wobbled my way towards the stage, which displayed a screenshot of someone named Katrina Lee Gorry. My stomach churned as I climbed the steps. Back at the table, Mum wondered at how tiny I looked on the enormous stage.

I'm used to crowds at games—they can spur you on in the most incredible way—but on those occasions you are one of eleven players (twenty-two if you count the opposition) running onto the ground and in the heat of combat. But here, in my little black frock and tottering heels, the spotlight was on little ol' me.

I couldn't remember what I said when I was handed the enormous silver trophy. Perhaps I should have listened to Mum because it all sounded like word vomit to me but, actually, based on what was reported in the media at the time, it sounded quite reasonable.

'I am absolutely ecstatic to win this award especially when up against such fantastic players in Aya Miyama and Nahomi Kawasumi. It really is an amazing honour. I think winning this award can help to serve as an inspiration for women's football in Australia and further the development which is growing rapidly, with bigger crowds and more media interest. The footballing talent of the younger girls who are coming through in Australia is crazy; we have so many quality players coming through and it's a challenge to keep your place in the Matildas line-up. The next six months ahead of the FIFA Women's World Cup are going to be exciting ones for Australian football.'

The Cinderella story ended at midnight. The next morning I was on my way back to Brisbane and the financial reality of my chosen career—a cafe job. I'm not complaining—I loved working there with Jade—but none of the regular customers had any idea that I played football, much less that I played for Australia and had won a major international award.

The next few days were a hoot as I fielded media calls between making coffee and serving pastries. Thankfully my boss was accommodating and gave me the time to step outside, sans hat and apron, to do interviews in the back lane.

It was so much easier a month later when I won the Professional Footballers Australia Women's Player of the Year. They told me via email; no ceremony, no dressing up. And I was right. My black gown has stayed encased in a plastic sleeve ever since, not because of fond memories so much as that I can't imagine another reason to wear it.

CHAPTER NINE

Benched

I'd love to introduce my first American experience as *The Wizard of Oz Goes to Kansas* but that would be over-egging the reality of my brief experience with the Kansas City Football Club. In fact, it felt more like Dorothy tripping innocently down the yellow brick road in her sparkly red shoes.

The deal was done in March, a few weeks after we'd finished the Australian domestic season and I had been named Brisbane's player of the year. There were four months between the Asian Cup final and the start of the next W-League season and it seemed a great opportunity to play in the top league in the United States.

It seemed that half the Matildas team would be over there as well. Sam Kerr and Lydia Williams were playing for Western New York Flash, Steph Catley for the Portland Thorns, Emily van Egmond the Chicago Red Stars (now

Chicago Stars), Lisa De Vanna the Boston Breakers and Caitlin Foord for Sky Blue (now NJ/NY Gotham) based in Jersey.

The press release put out by the Matildas on my behalf at the time expressed my positive feelings.

'I'm very excited about my signing with FC Kansas City. It will be an amazing experience mixing with and playing alongside some of the best players in the world. I've heard so many good things about the club and players so I'm really looking forward to getting over there.'

Kansas officials seemed just as excited. 'When we asked our players who they want on the team, Katrina's name came up several times,' the club's technical director, Huw Williams, was quoted as saying. 'That speaks volumes for her and, frankly, confirmed our thoughts that she could be a great fit for our team.'

But the reality was very different. I was twenty-one years old, on a high from my Asian Cup experience and naïve even to think that I could walk into the starting line-up for a prominent North American team which was chock-a-block full of senior domestic and international players the calibre of Amy Rodriguez, Lauren Holiday and Becky Sauerbrunn.

It was a shock to my ego because I'd rarely been picked as a bench player other than when I was being rested, and yet here in Kansas that's exactly what I was—a second-string player who may or may not get a run, let alone a significant role on the pitch.

Without the excitement of games to look forward to, life in rural Kansas was tedious to say the least; the endless routine of training, eating and recovery with nothing much in between. I lived by myself in a four-bedroom apartment and shut the doors to the other rooms because I hated being alone. Other team members lived nearby but there was very little socialising, particularly with the senior players who were a little older and had their own lives.

(As an aside, I'd like to mention the Engel family who were kind enough to lend me one of the family cars—appropriately a Mini Cooper—because I couldn't afford to rent a car for three months and needed to get around the city, which had minimal public transport. They answered an appeal I put out on social media. I'm so glad they didn't witness my initial attempts to drive a manual car on the right-hand side of the road, although the car and I both survived.)

The club's records show that I was selected in ten matches and only started in three, playing a total of 376 minutes during which I had seventeen shots at goal and scored once. But statistics don't tell the full story.

It was halfway through the season when I arrived in June, so it was unsurprising that I needed to find my way into a team that was already established. I had a promising beginning when I was included in the starting line-up against Houston Dash and got seventy-eight minutes before being subbed.

But I was relegated to the bench the following week and had to wait another month before getting my second start, against Portland, a match in which I scored. My only full ninety minutes on the field came against Sky Blue a few weeks later, and even then they played me out of position as a defensive wing.

In between times I was on the bench and brought on midway through the second half, not as a shock player injected into the game to make a difference, which I would have happily accepted, but to give a more senior player a rest. It was a role that my mindset found difficult to accept. I was desperate to find a way to get extra game time, but whenever I tried to talk to someone about it I hit a brick wall of indifference with little or no feedback.

The head coach, Vlatko Andonovski, who would later head the US national team, concentrated on his senior eleven players and had little to do with the rest of us, beyond telling me that I didn't fit the midfield set-up that he wanted. It seemed at times as if there were two teams—at least that's the way it felt to me.

I wasn't alone. Morgan Marlborough and Mandy Laddish were both promising players who had represented the USA at under-20 and under-23 levels. The three of us were in the same boat, rarely chosen in the starting line-up and spending matches simply sitting on the bench, fearing that we wouldn't be match-fit if called on during a game.

We bonded in our dejection, doing extra sessions after training and even getting matching tattoos of the three M's—Morgan, Mandy and Mini. They kept me sane in those three months because I simply couldn't get answers from the coaching staff about what I could do to improve. It's hard to keep your energy levels up when you don't feel part of a team, and towards the end of the season I had lost so much confidence that I began to hope that I wouldn't be called on at all, for fear of making a mistake.

I was young and had been flying in my career before I took the contract. The money, about US$25,000 as far as I recall, was not important to me. All I wanted to do was play, get better and test myself against the best players in the world.

But rather than gaining experience, I lost myself to some degree and began to feel as if everything I had achieved was slipping away. Instead of being eager to be competing against more senior players, and wanting to beat them and shine, I felt as if I didn't deserve to be out there with them at all.

Poor Mum spent hours on the phone with me, counselling and preaching patience as I bawled my eyes out and pleaded with her to book me a ticket on the next plane home. My twenty-second birthday on 13 August was drab.

'Nobody will even miss me or know that I've gone,' I wailed.

The team finished second in the regular season, then came back in the finals to win the championship title, beating favourites Seattle 2–1 in a terrific match in late August. I got a few minutes on the ground as a late substitution in the semi-final win over Portland but did not get a run at all in the final, listed as 'subs not used'.

A photograph of the team and its medal taken after the match shows me grinning in the front row, but the celebrations felt hollow, and I couldn't wait to get home. Mum had flown over for the final and we left the next day.

If there was a positive out of that tough situation then I would say that it made me even more determined to ensure that I played for a team who wanted me in their starting line-up, and to expect more from coaches and staff in how they communicate with *all* members of their roster.

There was one, unexpected plus from my Kansas experience. Midfielder Amy Rodriguez was returning to the game after having her first child. Her previous team, Seattle, had not renewed her contract and she was picked up instead by Kansas. She repaid their faith by top-scoring for us that season, including scoring two goals in the final to beat her former club.

Amy was older than me and so I didn't hang around her much outside the team, but she and Lauren Holiday were generous with their time at training. Amy would also be one of my inspirations later in deciding that I could have my own child while still playing.

CHAPTER TEN

So Near, and Yet…

The Matildas squad for the 2015 World Cup in Canada was officially confirmed in early May after four months of preparations, including a series of training camps at Australian Institute of Sport where we lived five days a week and went home on weekends.

By the time we travelled to Canada, we were probably the fittest we'd ever been, having played and trained with and against the AIS boys, as well as playing a number of friendlies. In the Cyprus Cup in March we'd also played some of the top-ranked teams like England and the Netherlands who stood between us and our best result at a World Cup.

There were few expectations on us, particularly after we'd been drawn in the so-called group of death alongside the USA (ranked second in the world), Sweden (ranked fifth) and Nigeria, who were the African champions. But being the underdog is a very comforting place because it allows you to concentrate on being together as a team and setting out to prove others wrong.

Staj described us as a 'positive squad', insisting that if we were to succeed then we had to go into every game with the belief we could win it. 'The emphasis has been on expressing our Australian culture and the things this country is renowned to bring to any sporting contest, things like positivity, back yourself and really taking it up to the opposition. Considering the other teams we have in our group, it brings this philosophy into even sharper focus.'

The game against the USA was a massive one for us in front of 32,000 mostly American fans. We were excited rather than fearful, despite never having beaten the US team in twenty-four games, but it was important to start the tournament positively, and there was no time for me to dwell on the fact that this was my first World Cup. I was here to play, not to stare in wonder.

We began well and it felt like we were on top of them and playing with confidence. It was only several great saves by their goalkeeper Hope Solo (now Stevens)—first denying Emily van Egmond whose shot from the edge of the area was tipped against the bar and then deflecting a stunning volley from Sam Kerr—that stopped us from taking an early lead.

Instead, and against the play, it was the USA who scored first through veteran Megan Rapinoe, who twisted and turned in the middle of a wall of our defenders before firing off a shot that got a deflection off Laura Alleway and gave goalkeeper Melissa Barbieri no chance as the ball spun and swerved into the far corner.

We responded fantastically and ten minutes later got our own chance when Michelle Heyman coolly laid off a ball at the top of the box to find Lisa De Vanna who smashed the ball into the net.

The team walked into the change rooms at half-time feeling pretty pleased with ourselves at 1–1. That was until we heard Abby Wambach, the US captain, loudly geeing up her teammates: 'That's okay girls, we're a second-half team.'

The mood in our rooms suddenly dulled. We'd all run our arses off for forty-five minutes just to kept pace with them. It was true that we could have been ahead, and we still didn't fear them, but the comment had planted the seed of doubts in our minds. I don't know if Staj heard the Wambach comment, but his message echoed the concern, praising our first-half performance but warning us we had to redouble our efforts in the second half if we were going to hold off the Americans.

As expected the second half was much more intense as the US team lifted their game and Rapinoe became dominant, setting up the US's second goal when she collected a long kick, slipped it to Sydney Leroux who raced down the wing before crossing the ball into the middle of the box where Christen Press placed a precise, first-time shot into the net. She then sealed the match when she latched onto the ball midfield, ran down the left wing before finishing in style with a left-foot shot across the goal into the right-hand side of the net.

It was hard to deny that the USA deserved their win, although the 3–1 scoreline was flattering, and a two-goal deficit made our job of qualifying much more difficult. Behind the scenes Staj was happy that we had not let the US dictate the pace of the game and pleaded with us not to soften our self-belief.

There was a four-day break between each game as we re-grouped in preparation for a must-win match against Nigeria, the first time the two nations had played against one another.

What they lacked in poise, the Africans made up for with their physicality and unpredictability, so we needed a far more disciplined approach to the game and to snuff out the chances of counter-attacks.

The 'Super Falcons', as they are known, were ranked thirty-third in the world but it was clear from their first-round match against fifth-ranked Sweden that they were resilient, twice falling behind before drawing the game 3–3. They had some great young players, like their forward Asisat Oshoala who played for Liverpool and had just been voted the BBC Women's Footballer of the Year.

The game was always going to be full of action as both sides had their chances in the first half before Lisa De Vanna, our co-captain, made a blistering run and got the ball into the middle where Kyah Simon clipped it neatly over the advancing goalkeeper.

It was a comforting 1–0 lead at half-time but we were in no position to rest, rather we needed to build on our lead—as good sides do—if we were going to advance in the tournament.

Our defence became more confident in the second half, defying the Nigerians who were getting more and more physical but probably less effective as we started to feel we had control of the game. Our patience paid off in the sixty-eighth minute when Kyah latched onto a well-weighted diagonal ball from Sam Kerr to beat the goalkeeper at the far post and give the team a solid lead.

Things got tense in the final twenty minutes as Nigeria tried everything to get back on terms, Sam Kerr even copping a nasty elbow to the face as we held our own and posted a much-needed 2–0 win.

When Sweden and the USA drew 0–0 in their game it meant we only had to draw against the Swedes to get through to the knockout rounds. Back in Australia there was growing interest in the World Cup as SBS committed resources to show the entire tournament.

We fancied ourselves against Sweden in the match played in Edmonton. Even though we had only ever beaten them once, the sides matched up pretty evenly, physically and tactically. We had extra speed upfront, with players like Lisa De Vanna who could trouble their defence.

Sweden's strength was their experience, with six players having played more than 100 internationals while only Lisa had reached 100 for the Matildas. The Swedes also had several X-factor players like their captain Caroline Seger and striker Sofia Jakobsson who could turn a game in a moment unless they were watched.

And that's how it panned out. We got off to a dream start when, in just the fifth minute, Laura Alleway floated a long-range ball over the heads of the Swedish defence where it was pounced on by Lisa who beat the offside trap and slotted the ball home in a one-on-one duel with the goalkeeper.

Sweden, as expected, hit back hard and Jakobsson got the equaliser just ten minutes later when she cut through our defence and hit a left-foot strike from just outside the box which dipped and curled to beat Lydia and sneak into the right-hand corner of the net. It wasn't their only chance in the first half as Lydia had to make two great saves to keep the game level at half-time.

The second half would turn into a grind as we held the Swedes at bay, knowing that a draw would be enough for us to reach the quarter-finals, something many commentators had thought unlikely before the tournament had begun.

With less than ten minutes left I was subbed off, somewhat reluctantly, and sat there as the tension grew.

When the final whistle went I ran back onto the field to celebrate with the others. We had survived the group of death.

———

I was happy with my own form at the World Cup, particularly defensively. I was probably the fittest and strongest I had ever been and concentrating hard on finding space so I could provide support and good connections through the midfield from defence into attack.

So I was surprised when Staj approached me a few days before the knockout game against Brazil, played in the city of Moncton on the east coast of Canada, to tell me that I was going to start on the bench. He wanted Tameka Butt on the field, specifically to mark their midfielder Formiga because he believed Tameka matched up better.

I hated coming off the bench 'to make an impact' and spent a couple of days moping and feeling sorry for myself. But Mum and Dad and Michelle, who had all come over to watch the World Cup, insisted that things would work out, so by game day I was at peace with the decision and ready to play my part. I sat next to Kyah Simon on the bench.

To progress past this game we had to do what no other senior Australian side had done: win a knockout match at a World Cup. And we had to do it against the team that had knocked us out of a previous World Cup. Could we defy history?

There were chances at both ends in the first half, including Formiga whose long-range shot forced a great save from Lydia Williams. At 0–0 we felt we were in the game at half-time and capable of breaking through.

The skies above Moncton opened up in the second half, and as the rain set in Brazil began to pile on the pressure, forcing Lydia to save several long-range bombs. We held firm and I fidgeted on the bench.

Kyah replaced Michelle Heyman after sixty-four minutes and I continued to sit there waiting for my chance. It came with barely twenty minutes left, replacing Tameka who'd worked hard and well to contain the dangerous Formiga.

'And on comes Katrina Gorry,' the television commentator proclaimed. 'What a great story she is; told that she was too small to ever play international football and yet here she is, playing for her country in the World Cup finals.'

I'd only been on the ground for a couple of minutes when an opportunity came my way. Lisa De Vanna had won a free kick on the left wing and the set-piece cross to the top of the box had been resisted by Brazil and fallen at my feet. I hit it first time but it was wide and a chance went begging. How many more would we get?

A few minutes later, I had another when I won possession of a disputed ball in the middle of the ground. I looked up to see a gap between two Brazilian defenders and space behind for Lisa De Vanna, who used her speed to run onto the ball and get a shot on goal. It was almost a replay of her goal against Sweden, as she guided the ball towards the left-hand post only for the keeper to block the shot as it bounced awkwardly in front of her. But instead of gathering, the keeper pushed the ball into the path of an oncoming Kyah

Simon who had followed up and now steered the ball into the net.

I was delirious. Mum and Dad and Michelle were on their feet in the stands.

'They are on the verge of history,' the commentator called excitedly. 'What a moment for Australian women's football.'

We managed to hold on for the next ten minutes against an increasingly desperate Brazil, thanks to some great saves by Lydia. When the final whistle went there was pandemonium as we realised what we had achieved.

The biggest controversy during the tournament was the use of artificial grass pitches which many players thought were dangerous, 'like walking on hot coals', as Michelle said in one media interview.

In the hour before our quarter-final against Japan, played back in Edmonton, an American sports commentator measured the air temperature on the ground at twenty-eight degrees and the turf temperature at sixty-six degrees.

It might have seemed a warmish afternoon for people sitting in the stands watching the action but out there on the artificial grass it was horrendous. I've never been so struck by heat as we ran out onto the ground where we were determined to press the Japanese midfield to give them less time on the ball and make it more difficult for them to rely on their passing skills.

We achieved our aim in the first half, restricting them to five attempts on goal, only one of which was on target, even though they had sixty per cent possession. At the break, Staj kept insisting that it wasn't that bad out there, but it *was*, and there were no drinks breaks because the air temperature hadn't reached thirty-two degrees.

Despite the conditions, both sides lifted the tempo in the second half as we tried to shift the emphasis from chasing Japanese shadows to creating more chances for ourselves. We swapped speed for height midway through the half when Larissa Crummer came on for Lisa De Vanna and then, with fifteen minutes to go, Staj brought on more height by replacing me with Michelle Heyman. Watching the game later I could see I looked exhausted as I came off.

As the minutes ticked by, television commentators began telling their viewers that the match was likely to go to extra time, but with just three minutes left, the Japanese broke our hearts when they scored from a goalmouth scramble: 1–0. Our run had come to an end.

Staj was circumspect at the post-match media conference. He did not blame the heat: 'They had more chances. The better team won on the day,' he conceded, sipping from a bottle of water.

One American journalist had noticed how upset we all were after the game. 'Your players looked devastated. What did you say to them?'

'There's not much you can say after a game like that other than put your arm around their shoulders,' Staj said. 'They're all very young. Sometimes it's what you learn from these bad experiences that can mean the most.'

There was one more question, this time from an Australian journalist who wanted to know if Australia should be doing more to keep the players together as a group: 'Is Japan the sort of team you should aspire to?'

'Yes.' Staj smiled. 'It's all about process and that doesn't happen overnight. You said we've been full-time but it's only been five months. The Japanese girls have been together for five, six, ten years. They're all around thirty and have already won a World Cup, an Asian Cup and silver at the Olympics, and you can tell why. Their chemistry is fantastic, they're technically superb. The bulk of our starting line-up are twenty-one or twenty-two. We'll get there. We've got a great base from which to work. By the time the Olympics come around next year we want to take some more steps forward.'

CHAPTER ELEVEN

Taking a Stand for Equality

We all scattered after the World Cup was over and the USA had triumphed against Japan 5–2. Some players went to Europe, others remained in North America and returned to their clubs to finish the domestic season, and the rest of us returned to Australia where we received something of a hero's welcome.

More than 350,000 people had watched our quarter-final against Japan on SBS television, one of forty-one matches the station had telecast live during a World Cup which had attracted one million unique viewers on its website.

A key moment in the history of women's sport had happened because a media company had decided to put aside commercial gain for fairness and showcase women's sport at its best—whether it was watched or not.

Although no one could have known, it was the first taste of the Matildas excitement that was to come in the 2023 World Cup.

'We didn't decide to show the whole tournament to gain huge viewing figures or garner some sort of commercial success,' SBS announced. 'We did it because it was the right thing to do.'

The argument that people weren't interested in women's sport had been shown to be complete bullshit, not only in Australia but in America where previous viewing records had been smashed, and the UK where the English team, the Lionesses, had become hugely popular.

And yet, for all this success, we were about to become embroiled in one of the worst off-field moments in my career.

It just so happened that our playing contracts had expired during the World Cup, and behind the scenes there had already been some rather angry discussions going on between the Professional Footballers' Association and Football Federation Australia about fair pay.

The situation had been a minor distraction for the players during the tournament. I was even asked about it by a journalist but I had said we were concentrating on winning the tournament, not our pay packets. That was true to a point. But this was about our financial futures.

Under our now expired contracts, which had been negotiated in 2011 before I was selected, we were regarded as semi-professional players who were paid A$21,000 a year to be a member of the national team. The minimum wage in Australia at the time was a little over $34,000.

In the six months leading up to the World Cup we were expected to attend nine separate training camps and play fifteen 'friendlies' across Asia and Europe. It was a heavy schedule, as you would expect, but it meant that during this time our jobs (all of us had to find work outside football), studies and family commitments had to be put aside. It later turned out that some of my team-mates even had to resort to receiving welfare benefits just to make ends meet.

On top of that base figure, we were paid $500 for each international match and a scale of fees for tournaments—group games, quarter-finals, semi-finals and finals—depending on how well we played. Our match fee for playing the quarter-final of the World Cup against Japan was $750. By comparison, the men's team, the Socceroos, earned $6500 for an international match and $9500 for playing in a quarter-final.

Was that fair? We didn't think so.

Despite the obvious inequality, being involved in a pay dispute was not a comfortable situation for many of the players. None of us had expected to become rich playing football. We played because we loved the game and were proud to represent our country. It may sound over-the-top to some people, but standing in the middle of the ground with my team-mates and listening to the national anthem makes me emotional. I have cried on a number of occasions; real tears, real emotion because my only desire has ever been to be in a Matildas shirt and winning the World Cup or the Olympic Games. It still is!

I had made a decision to pursue a career as a professional footballer knowing that it was not likely that I was going to be able to afford to buy a house any time soon. I was young and excited and didn't need lots of money, other than to buy the best boots, of course.

When I wasn't training or playing for the Matildas or Brisbane Roar, I was working in a cafe or, later, as an office receptionist at a school where they were very understanding and gave me the flexibility to take time to tour with the team.

In 2012, I had taken the contract to play for Ottawa Fury to get overseas experience knowing there was no payment other than being given a place to stay and my uniforms. Mum and Dad paid the airfares. I was given food vouchers for pizzas and Subway sandwiches—hardly high-performance food—and the occasional bag of groceries as well as entry once a week into a nearby restaurant that served pasta. I had no time to take a part-time job and lived off my minimal savings and the generosity of my family.

I didn't complain then and I'm not complaining now. It was the way things were and I was prepared to make those sacrifices to do the thing that I had loved since the age of six when I refused to play netball and insisted on playing football. I regard myself as fortunate to have had a passion to pursue in life. I am glad I made those decisions and I have no regrets.

But if ever things were going to change for the better then it was in August 2015 when the Matildas had returned from our excellent World Cup in Canada, with the best wishes of then Prime Minister Tony Abbott, and a level of public acknowledgement and respect we had never experienced before.

Everyone was proud of what we had achieved. We were gritty and determined and fun to watch, and people wanted us to do well and become the best team in the world. But unless we could become full-time, professional players with the right support and development then that was not going to happen.

A fortnight after we had returned to Australia it was announced that the Matildas would travel to the USA in September and play two matches, in Detroit and Birmingham, Alabama, against the new world champions as part of their national tour celebration.

It was exciting news, given that the stadiums in both cities quickly sold out and we would play each match in front of more than 30,000 people. The matches would also be televised in America and back in Australia—a dream publicity opportunity and chance to show that we were a side that could match the best in the world.

Surely the pay dispute would be resolved in the meantime, particularly as we had not been paid in two months. The Football Federation had proposed a deal to almost double our basic contract to $40,000 a year, but the best offer the FFA chief executive David Gallop had put forward was a ten per cent rise over four years, to a paltry $23,000. And yet they wanted us to get on a plane and travel to America where national team players were each earning around $200,000 a year, including a base rate of $70,000.

It wasn't just about money. We wanted basic minimum standards setting out timing commitments and requirements. I was particularly keen on this paragraph:

Establishing a career pathway for elite women footballers and making football the sport of choice for young women.

There also needed to be an improvement in our travelling conditions and accommodation standards. Up until this time we'd had to fit within a budget that made travel cramped and difficult at times and we stayed in some really shitty hotels where most of us washed our underwear in the sink. We were supposed to be elite athletes arriving in good health to play international sporting events, not backpackers on a shoestring budget.

I had been on tours through Asia where the hotels were so bad that some of the girls wouldn't eat anything but boiled rice and protein drinks because of the poor state of hotel kitchens, which stank and were full of cockroaches. In other hotels, players found it difficult to sleep because beds were rock hard or the sheets didn't look as if they had been regularly changed.

Airlines were another issue. We were sometimes forced to take flights because they were the cheapest rather than the best to suit our schedule. I remember one sequence in the weeks before the World Cup which typified the problem. We had been in a training camp in Italy after playing in the Cyprus Cup in March when two matches were hurriedly arranged—one against Austria and the other against Scotland.

It was snowing when we flew into the city of Villach for the Austrian game. We arrived at one o'clock in the morning and were taken to our hotel. The match, which we lost 2–1, was scheduled for 2 pm that day after which we were driven straight back to the airport and flown later that night to the town of Falkirk, Scotland, for another match the following day. We drew 1–1. Neither match made us better players, just more tired and prone to injury.

Flying economy class on the long-haul flights to and from Australia is not conducive to an athlete's wellbeing. I'm tiny so it doesn't bother me much to fold myself into an economy-class seat, but some of the other players were finding it very difficult, physically, to arrive and play at their best. Being cramped niggles injuries that we all nurse through a season, and sleep is difficult for many people when you can't stretch out. We are not tourists when we travel overseas; we are travelling to work and perform—just like politicians and CEOs.

And yet some sections of the media, including some women journalists writing columns for newspapers, accused us of being ungrateful prima donnas: 'Demanding business-class airfares and five-star accommodation goes against what we love about these women.'

It all came to a head on 9 September, the day before the team was due to fly out for a training camp. We all flew into Sydney with our bags packed. The PFA encouraged us all to go down with our suitcases emblazoned with the Australian motif to the FFA offices in Oxford Street to meet and discuss the issue. But the media was waiting for us. Someone had tipped them off.

The whole thing looked like a confrontation when it wasn't. We genuinely believed that we were meeting David Gallop and that the whole issue would be decided so we could go to the airport and get on the plane. But he wasn't there.

It was a surreal moment. Photographs taken later show us standing around in Hyde Park looking lost and sad (I looked angry) as we were waiting for updates being telephoned to us from our association representatives inside.

When it became obvious that the stalemate would continue, and that all we were being offered was a temporary payment to cover the American matches while the negotiations dragged on, we had only one option—to boycott the tour.

It seemed unthinkable, but the Matildas would go on strike. No one wanted to say 'no' to representing Australia—it felt like we were letting everyone down—but we had been driven to a point where we had to make a stand or else nothing would ever change.

The players had kept in touch with a few of our American counterparts, some of whom now openly supported our stance, including goalkeeper Hope Solo and captain Abby Wambach, who said:

'What the Australian women are doing is they're empowering themselves and they're empowering the next generation of women coming behind them to stand up and speak up for what is right and what they think that they deserve. We did this many, many years ago and us, as players, are now reaping the rewards.'

The one vocal objector from within the team was our captain, Lisa De Vanna, who expressed her frustrations in a media interview: 'I just want to play for my country. It's all I want to do. If my coach calls me and asks me to play I will always make myself available. At my age I am not sure if the opportunity to play the world champions will come up again.'

Some of my team-mates were angry about Lisa's position. Personally, I had no problem with Lisa. I understood where she was coming from. Like all of us, she was a person driven to succeed. The difference was that there are times when the team comes before the individual, and the future comes before the present. This, I believe, was one of those times.

Haiti replaced us for the American games and got clobbered 8–0 and 5–0. It wasn't the 'Victory Tour' spectacle the USA had wanted but 70,000 fans still turned up to witness the ritual dissection of a team ranked sixty-third in the world. We would have given the US team a run for their money.

Back in Sydney, it would take the FFA barely a month to relent and by early November we had a new package under which the top players received a base salary of $41,000 and a second tier under which players received $30,000. There were also improved match payments and a daily allowance for players during training camps as well as commitments about career paths for young women.

The players had happily ended the strike before the deal was finalised and in early October the Matildas were reunited for the first time since the World Cup in preparation for a fleeting visit to China where we would play the host nation and England (we drew 1–1 with China and went down 0–1 to England) ahead of the 2016 Rio Olympics, now barely eight months away.

Despite the deal, we were still semi-professional because most of us continued to rely on part-time jobs to make a living. But the new payment deal was a huge step forward for the game and would pave the way for subsequent improvements as the game continued to grow. I would have celebrated with a new pair of boots but that had changed as well, as sponsors suddenly came calling as Matildas' merchandise was becoming more popular than the Socceroos'.

By February 2016, with the pay dispute a fading bitter memory, the serious business began again as we travelled to Osaka for the Asian Football Confederation's Olympic qualification tournament. We hadn't competed at the Games since Athens in 2004, always falling at the hurdle of the qualification tournament. And free-to-air television would, for the first time, telecast the matches live.

It was a difficult task to qualify through Asia because there were six teams vying for only two slots available. Now ranked ninth by FIFA, we had to get past Japan (4), North (6) and South Korea (18) and China (17) if we were going to make it to the Brazil Olympics.

Japan was our first and biggest target with both sides fielding the same starting line-up from our World Cup quarter-final match. This time it was the Matildas who were quicker and more accurate, surprising Japan with our pressure, as their star player Miyama Aya later conceded: 'We weren't fully ready.'

For once we felt in control against a side that had previously bamboozled us with their clinical passing, particularly in midfield where I was on my game, responsible for the cross in the twenty-fifth minute that Lisa De Vanna latched onto to give us a 1–0 lead. I later scored with a rare header of my own, nodding the ball home at the far post from a fabulous cross by Emily van Egmond. In between Michelle Heyman scored to give us a 3–1 victory.

With just two days' rest, we thumped Vietnam 9–0 before a showdown with the two Koreas—South first, who we beat 2–0 thanks to Kyah Simon and Emily van Egmond—and then North who were as tough and mysterious as the forbidding nation. It was a match that would be watched by almost 400,000 back home in Australia.

Michelle Heyman scored early and the two sides battled for the next hour before North Korea got an equaliser through a fantastic strike by Kim Su-Gyong. With six minutes to go, I was in the mix again, this time when Kyah Simon crossed the ball to Caitlin Foord who laid it back to me as I stood, unguarded, at the top of the box. My eyes lit up as I let fly with a strike into the left-hand corner.

I whooped down the field and leaped into Caitlin's arms as the whole team jumped for joy, realising it was the goal that sealed our tickets to Rio. 'They're not dreaming anymore,' the commentator yelled as the final whistle went. 'They're back on the Olympic stage after twelve long years. Look what it means to them.'

We may have secured the Rio prize but the tournament was still there to be won as we faced China two days later, who had also beaten Japan. A hard-fought 1–1 draw, thanks to an eighty-fifth-minute goal to Emily van Egmond gave us our first piece of silverware since the 2010 Asian Cup.

CHAPTER TWELVE
Ecstasy and Agony

Which tournament would I rather win—a World Cup or an Olympic Games?

It's a tough question. Most players would say a World Cup because it's our biggest tournament and the epitome of our sport, but I didn't watch much football on TV when I was growing up. The Olympics every four years was something special though. We all grew up wanting to be an Olympian.

Whenever the Olympics was on, I watched virtually every sport—I loved them all—and got chills when I watched a medal ceremony and heard the Aussie anthem. So if I had to choose then an Olympic title would be my choice. I guess I'll only know when and if it happens.

One of the mementos I treasure most is a ticket stub for my seat aboard a Qantas flight to Rio de Janeiro. The flight number states *Aus Olympic Team* and the details say it is a flight from Australia to the Rio 2016 Olympic Games. It has no seat number because we were all flying together and decided our seating when we got onboard.

'Best feeling in the world', I wrote on Instagram with a photo of the ticket.

But that feeling didn't last long. In our first game, we let in the fastest ever goal in Olympic history. You could not imagine a worse start to the tournament. A defensive error, just twenty-one seconds into the game at the Arena Corinthians, allowed Canadian captain Christine Sinclair to intercept and arrow a precise pass to team-mate Janine Beckie, who tapped the ball into the net from barely one metre out.

Things seemed to go our way twenty minutes later when Michelle Heyman was grappled and brought down as she headed towards goal. The Canadian tackler was red-carded and sent off, leaving Canada with just ten players for the seventy minutes that remained.

With that advantage, surely we could score twice to win the game? But, despite peppering their goal, we couldn't find a way through the Canadian defence, and when they counter-attacked in the final minutes, Lydia Williams was caught out near the halfway line as Canada cleared their lines. Sinclair latched onto the ball and launched a long-range shot over Lydia's head for a second goal.

We'd had twenty-two shots on goal, including twelve on target, compared to Canada's eight and four, and yet we'd failed to score. Poor Michelle had to front the media on behalf of the team: 'It's heart-breaking and devastating . . . and I'm disappointed in myself,' she told the journalists.

There was no doubt that it was a serious setback for our campaign but I knew we could bounce back. I wrote on Twitter:

Nothing can break this family 💪 *Not the way we wanted to start our Olympic campaign but now it's time to refocus, recover and prepare for Germany.*

How things can turn. In the next game, against Germany, Sam Kerr gave us the lead after just five minutes, thanks to a bustling run by Caitlin Foord. As Caitlin charged through the centre of the field, she picked out Sam, who finished clinically with her left foot from ten metres out.

Caitlin then scored herself just before half-time after Lisa De Vanna chased down a through ball, nutmegged a defender and cleverly picked out Caitlin who had positioned herself in front of goal. I'd been nursing a knock on the knee a few minutes earlier but any nagging pain disappeared as I sprinted down the ground as support behind Caitlin and watched her turn the ball into the goal.

But our hopes of going into half-time with a 2–0 lead evaporated a minute later in extra time when midfielder Sara Däbritz used the outside of her left foot to dink the ball over Lydia Williams. It hit the underside of the crossbar and went in to bring the Germans back into the game.

It had been a pulsating half as both sides pressed to score. Lydia made several great saves, as did the German keeper, including one of my long-range strikes. The second half continued in the same vein but the 2–1 scoreline in our favour did not change until, with three minutes left, Germany won a dubious free kick on the left flank. The ball was swung into the back post where, somehow, their centre back Saskia Bartusiak chested the ball into the goal to pinch a last-gasp draw.

It was another blow to our campaign. Now, rather than a guaranteed slot in the finals, we faced the possibility of an early exit from the tournament unless we could beat Zimbabwe by a large margin.

In that game, at Itaipava Fonte Nova, we dominated Zimbabwe for ninety minutes. Lisa De Vanna settled our nerves by scoring in the first two minutes, followed by Clare Polkinghorne ten minutes later and then Alanna Kennedy leaped high to make it three by half-time.

Kyah Simon's first-time strike made it 4–0 early in the second half and then my roomie Michelle Heyman came onto the field to score twice, first a header at the far post and then a neat strike after beating Zimbabwe's offside trap. We'd slammed in six goals, but we needed a seventh goal to finish the pool matches in second position. This would be better than finishing as the best-placed third side, which would result in a knockout clash with the tournament hosts Brazil. But our constant pressing left us open to a counter-attack and it was the Africans who took advantage and scored in the ninety-first minute.

Our hopes of an easier run through the knockout phase were dashed. We would have to face Brazil.

The day of our quarter-final clash happened to be my twenty-fourth birthday. Surely it was a sign that we were going to win and create not only a new record for Australian football—men or women—by reaching a semi-final but also elevate the sport to a new level in Australia.

As it turned out, it would be one of the most important, memorable and challenging days of my life as more than 50,000 people packed into the stadium.

It was almost a dream start as I latched onto the ball after just one minute, stepped forward and had a flying shot at goal towards the top right-hand corner. But their goal-keeper, Barbara, anticipated my aim. It wouldn't be the last time that Barbara and I would face off that night.

Brazil looked very dangerous early and when Lydia Williams stretched wide to block a swinging strike by Debinha it seemed like just a matter of time before they would score. But we began to settle and held firm as the first half progressed, even making a few forays forward ourselves. We were pleased to get in at half-time with the match in the balance.

We began much better in the second half with Sam Kerr and Michelle Heyman both having good attempts thwarted. Tempers began to fray as the minutes ticked down, with a flurry of poor tackles and injury delays. For Brazil, Tamires, Marta and Andressa Alves were shown yellow cards while Caitlin Foord and Alanna Kennedy also transgressed.

Our best chance came with just four minutes of regular time remaining when I stole the ball from the feet of their tall forward Beatriz Zaneratto in the centre of the ground. I turned and spied Caitlin in space at the top of the box. She took my pass cleanly and laid it back to Chloe Logarzo who let fly with a long-range shot. She was unlucky to hit the crossbar.

It was 0–0 at full-time so we headed into thirty minutes of extra time. This is where my endurance begins to pay dividends. Two minutes in and I got another opportunity as we surged forward out of defence. I dropped into the top of the box where Caitlin found me and I struck it first time, just wide and into the side netting.

Neither side seemed to be slowing. Brazil was again looking very dangerous but they were unable to score. I had another shot which was blocked. The last fifteen minutes were exhausting but the pace of the match remained high as the ball went from end to end. I reckon the crowd, large and noisy, was as drained by the on-field drama as we were.

Caitlin just missed another shot and, with two minutes left, Brazil's chief playmaker, Marta, charged down the left-hand side, wrong-footed one of our defenders and forced a great Lydia Williams' save as she turned the shot around the post.

Penalties would have to decide who would go through to the semi-finals.

We'd all been practising penalties in the weeks leading up to the Olympics. I was pretty confident from the spot, although I would never expect to be called on to take a penalty during normal game time.

The decision on which five players will take the initial penalty kicks is never made until the final whistle is blown because you never know how a match will progress, and the manager can only choose from the eleven players who are left on the ground at the end. In this case, Sam Kerr would not take a penalty kick because she had been substituted late in the game.

Our coach, Alen Stajcic, walked around our group looking at his clipboard and then pointing at players. Elise Kellond-Knight would take our first kick, followed by Laura Alleway, Emily van Egmond and Clare Polkinghorne.

'You're number five,' Staj said jabbing his finger in my direction. I nodded but said nothing. On the television screen I looked calm but I can tell you that my heart was thumping. I took a deep breath.

The players stood at the halfway line and linked arms. I was at the end, Michelle on my left with her arm around my shoulder while I put my arm around her waist, our faces set in stone as we waited. The Brazilians, to my right, were doing the same. There was little chatter among us, most of us lost in private thoughts and anxieties about what the next few minutes would bring—joy for one side, devastation for the other.

Brazil won the toss and would take the first kick. Their midfielder Andressa wasted no time when the whistle blew, giving Lydia Williams no chance by sending her the wrong way and hammering the ball into the right-hand corner. Andressa leaped, pulled her shirt with pride and punched the air with delight as the hometown crowd erupted: 1–0 Brazil.

Elise stepped forward and calmly slotted the ball into the right-hand corner. Her unemotional response to the successful kick as she walked back to our group was in stark contrast to Andressa. I also noticed that, unlike Lydia, their goalkeeper Barbara had been moving forward as the kick was taken, a tactic used to cut down the angle. I could see it from where I stood and the television replays would show that she was two metres in front of her line and in the air as the kick went flying past.

Was this legal, given that the law says that one foot must be on the goal line when the kick is taken? The goal counted anyway so no action was taken: 1–1.

Brazil's Andressinha was next and this time Lydia guessed correctly and got a hand to the low and powerful shot but couldn't keep it out of the left-hand netting: 2–1 Brazil.

Laura hesitated for a moment before repeating Andressinha's kick and burying the ball into the left-hand corner. Barbara, who had moved early again, got fingers to the ball and thumped the ground in frustration when it went in: 2–2.

Unlike her team-mates, Beatriz did not try to blast the ball but steered it high and to the left. Lydia guessed correctly but could do nothing to stop it: 3–2 Brazil.

There was now no doubt about Barbara's goalkeeping tactics, as Emily stepped forward and slotted it into the bottom right-hand corner. The goalkeeper, who was clearly two metres off her line when Emily struck the ball, had gone the other way: 3–3.

Brazil's left-footers continued with Rafaelle who converted to the bottom right-hand corner and charged off to celebrate, a la Andressa: 4–3 Brazil. Clare was equally calm as she copied Emily's tactic and placed it to the right-hand side: 4–4.

Brazil's captain, Marta, stepped up. The five-time world player of the year (she would later win it a sixth time) looked nervous, glancing left and right as she approached the spot. Was she genuinely undecided about which way to go or was she trying to confuse Lydia? Lydia would reveal later that she had studied Marta's penalty-taking record in the lead-up to the game, just in case this situation arose.

Marta settled, ran in and struck the ball low and left. Lydia guessed correctly, her right hand reaching out to touch the ball and keep it out. I was the first to react, bouncing forward with glee as Marta hid her face in her shirt in disappointment. The crowd was silent: 4–4.

It was up to me. If I converted, it would send the Matildas through to the semi-final and perhaps Olympic glory. I steeled myself and walked forward to the spot, deciding in that moment that I was going to send the ball to the left corner with the natural swing of my foot. I avoided looking at the goalkeeper.

As I struck it, Barbara was already one metre off her line and moving to her right, blocking the ball with both hands and sending the crowd into a frenzy. I let out a frustrated puff, turned and walked back to the line.

I had missed, unaware of Barbara's obvious foul. The assistant referee, standing on the goal line with a clear view, did not move even though she had seen Barbara use the same tactic with every other kick. I later saw the media reports with very clear photos of the positions of both the goalkeeper and the assistant referee. The law says that the penalty should have been retaken and Barbara warned. Instead, the score remained 4–4.

It was now sudden death.

Four of the Brazilian players were on their knees at halfway as Debinha took her time before slotting it right-footed into the bottom left-hand side of the net: 5–4 Brazil.

Michelle Heyman, who now had to score to keep us in the tournament, looked composed and placed it high and right. Barbara, despite repeating her movement, could not reach it: 5–5.

Brazil's Monica went left—6–5—and so did Chloe Logarzo—6–6—while Tamires, a left footer, smashed it high into the top right corner: 7–6.

Alanna Kennedy struck the ball perfectly, high and right, and stood in disbelief as Barbara threw herself in the air and parried it away. Television replays showed she had begun moving forward and towards the left even before Alanna had taken her kick. It was clearly a foul but the assistant referee's flag stayed down.

The crowd erupted at the victory as Alanna stood with her face in her hands, crying. Clare was inconsolable, Chloe and Emily hugged and brave Lydia wept on the shoulder of a Brazilian player. I walked around the gathered players, unable to look at anyone, as the crowd burst into song and the Brazilians celebrated by taking selfies.

In the aftermath social media exploded about Barbara's goalkeeping but, as Staj would say, it was now all history.

'I thought the new rule was you should get a yellow card instantly for that kind of action but she didn't get one and then she proceeded to fudge that rule as much as she could. We're shattered but, in the cold light of day, as a coach and a staff, and I guess as a country, we're all extremely proud of the performance of the players and the resilience they showed—the courage and toughness. It's pretty raw at the moment. You can appreciate the effort the players have put in.'

But I would find it almost impossible to put it behind me. How could I when I had the chance to send us into the semi-final but missed? And now we had lost.

I had failed. I wasn't good enough. How would I ever recover?

CHAPTER THIRTEEN

Seeing Red

I can be mouthy at times on the pitch, particularly over what I see as bad refereeing, and in July 2016, on the eve of the Rio Olympic Games, my vocal exuberance came back to bite me.

We were playing our last warm-up game before the real action began, a friendly against the hosts Brazil. The match had no bearing on anything other than a potential psychological edge over one of our main rivals if we were to fulfil a dream and medal at the Games.

We had been on top in the first half and walked into the change rooms with a well-deserved 1–0 lead after a goal to Larissa Crummer. The only downer was that I had copped a yellow card for a poor tackle, so Staj warned me to take it easy in the second half. Unfortunately, my mouth got the better of me soon after the restart when the ref made a bad call. The ref didn't appreciate my response and showed me a second yellow card, which gave me an automatic red card.

I was sent off and it turned the game on its head—Brazil taking full advantage of us being a player down to score three times and run out comfortable winners. Receiving a red card means you are also suspended for the next game so I feared that I would miss our opening game against Canada a week later, but I was soon told that the Olympics did not come under the control of FIFA and so my suspension would be held over.

Fast-forward nine months, to March 2017, and the Matildas were in Portugal, having been a late invitation to play in the Algarve Cup. We had only played in this long-running tournament once before—way back in 1999—so this was an unlikely but welcome opportunity to come together for the first time since Brazil.

The Algarve Cup has a unique and quirky formula which divides the twelve competing teams into three groups that play each other in a round-robin formula. The two teams scoring the most points in the group stage then play off for the gold medal while the other group-stage winner plays off for bronze against the highest second-placed group team.

A bit strange, some would say, because your chances depend almost entirely on who you draw in the group stage, and we drew three tough opponents—Sweden, the Netherlands and China.

Sweden was first up—an old foe against whom we had slugged out ten draws in sixteen matches and only won twice—and I was out of the team to serve the Brazil suspension.

Staj was still fuming about the red card and had made me do run-and-shoot extras after training the previous day. They were killers and I remember thinking that I never wanted to get sent off again.

On match day I could only watch from the stands, frustrated and away from the team, as we held sway in the first half but missed a great chance to go ahead when Sam Kerr coasted past two defenders and found Kyah Simon who blazed her shot over the bar.

Sweden regrouped in the second half and almost scored several times before their captain Lotta Schelin broke the deadlock after charging down the right side, beating a defender and finishing on a tight angle.

We pressed hard for an equaliser but our attacks were mostly disjointed, apart from a cracking strike by Kyah with twenty minutes to go which was tipped over the bar by their goalkeeper. One last chance fell to Sam who tried to chip over the head of the keeper who, somehow, got a hand to the ball and deflected it wide.

I was back in the side for the second match, against the Netherlands just two days later—my fiftieth match for the Matildas and also Alanna Kennedy's fiftieth. It was a must-win if we wanted to have a chance to progress to the finals, but it was the Dutch who started better, and it was only the smart reflexes of Lydia Williams in goal that saved us from going behind.

After weathering the attacks, we broke the deadlock when an attacking run by Caitlin Foord earned a corner. A set-piece delivery reached Emily Gielnik who caught out their goalkeeper by curling the ball over her head and inside the far post. Just ten minutes later it happened again when Emily took a free kick and again curled it past a helpless goalkeeper as it found the top right-hand corner of the net.

It became 3–0 when Alanna celebrated her milestone with a thumping header from a curling Steph Catley free kick. The match seemed to be ours at half-time and we continued in the same vein after the break with Sam Kerr, Lisa De Vanna, Caitlin and myself all getting shots away in dangerous positions.

But the Netherlands almost made us pay for our misses when they scored twice inside the last fifteen minutes. In a dramatic last few moments we had to rely on the safe hands of Lydia Williams to hold them out.

China had lost their matches against Sweden and the Netherlands so our clash against the Asian powerhouse on Monday would decide our tournament fate.

It would not be an easy match, as they sat back with a tight 4–4–2 set-up to frustrate our attacking style and speed, and then played counter-attacking football—a tactic that was rewarded when their striker, Wang Shanshan, scored midway through the half.

We were peppering the goal and dominating possession but could not break through the Chinese structured defence until the sixty-first minute when Emily Gielnik, who had come on as a substitute, found the net.

From then on it seemed just a matter of time before we scored again as we had eighteen shots on goal and made almost twice as many passes as our opponents. Ellie Carpenter eventually scored the winner as she headed home an Emily van Egmond corner—her first goal for the Matildas.

It was a solid performance, and with the Netherlands scoring a surprise 1–0 win over Sweden in the other pool match, it meant we had finished top of our group with six points. But the tournament's unique format meant that the other group winners, Spain and Canada, qualified for the final with seven points from their games.

We faced off against Denmark for third place and, for a change, it was us who began the better side, creating a number of chances. When I went past two defenders down the left-hand side and found Kyah in the middle, she smashed the ball home at close range.

It was a tight contest and the two sides traded our minimal chances for the rest of the game until the last few minutes when their captain and star striker Pernille Harder controlled a long ball superbly, cut past two defenders and found the top right corner of the net. I had been assigned to mark Pernille for most of the game; we knew what she was capable of doing and she could slip from the number 10 role into the striker position easily, which is exactly what she did.

It was a deflating moment, and because there was no extra time in the tournament rules, we went straight to a penalty shootout. It was my nightmare after my Rio penalty miss, and I told Staj that I wasn't ready to take a kick.

In the shootout, Elise Kellond-Knight found the net, but Clare Polkinghorne and Sam Kerr both tried the left-hand corner and their shots were saved by the Danish goalkeeper Stina Lykke Borg. Denmark won 4–1.

A disturbing pattern was developing that had to be addressed if we were going to win an international tournament and be a threat at the World Cup.

CHAPTER FOURTEEN

Sushi and Ink Don't Mix

'Respect'. It's the word I associate with the Japanese and the way they approach not just their football but their lives. I first experienced this in 2012 when I made my debut for the Matildas and the crowd in the Tokyo grandstand high-fived me and Mum after the match. Two years later, when I guarded the Japanese captain Aya Miyama in the Asian Cup final, she bowed to me after the match and we swapped shirts before she ran off to celebrate with her team-mates.

So, in April 2017, when I was offered a try-out with a Japanese team in the Nadeshiko League, I jumped at the chance. I loved the idea of spending time in this amazing country and learning more about its society and values, not to mention the lure of the skills and playing style of Japanese football.

Caitlin Foord had been contracted to play for the Mynavi Sendai Ladies team, based in the city of Sendai, 400 kilometres north of Tokyo, and the club offered me a trial. I came prepared to stay, and thankfully did so for the next three months in what turned out to be one of my most treasured experiences.

I had some other very special but frustrating news around the same time. Jade Saunders, my closest friend, was getting married to her long-term girlfriend. It had always been an unwritten commitment between us that we would be there for each other's weddings but her ceremony was set for 6 August on the Sunshine Coast, just as the Japanese season entered the finals and the Matildas were due to play in a major tournament in the USA.

It was important to me that I find a way to attend the wedding—even if I had to fly out straight after a game—but Jade was also understanding and supportive of my career.

Japan is a country where everything is small and neat and built for purpose. Just like me! In fact, when I first had problems finding boots that fitted me properly, I used to order them from Japan.

My apartment echoed this idea. Unlike the acres of space of the almost empty four-bedroom flat I endured in Kansas, this time I had a tiny apartment where everything slotted into a space not much bigger than my bedroom. Caitlin lived in the same block, as did American player Brittany Cameron who was in her fourth season at Sendai and was a great help when it came to dealing with language barriers.

Rather than feeling claustrophobic, I found this way of living—simply and without fuss—a joy. Our Japanese team-mates lent us bits of furniture we needed for the apartments, I slept on the floor on a futon bed and I cooked on a tiny burner stove and in an oven, a bit like an air fryer. I didn't need many clothes, which was a refreshing change. I didn't even have a television set, although Japanese programs would have been a challenge anyway.

In the streets outside I felt safe and welcome, whether it was going out in the morning for a coffee and seeing the footpaths filled with little kids walking to school—something you are unlikely to witness in Australia where we drive everywhere—or going out at night for a meal at a nearby restaurant. I could walk down the street alone at 2 am and feel perfectly safe. They were the sort of streets where people stop to say hello rather than put their head down and scurry past. It was another example of the respect I felt.

Caitlin felt the same way. She wrote about her experiences a few years later, saying Japan was the place that surprised her most: 'I was there with Matildas team-mate Katrina Gorry and we explored as much as we could to really soak in the culture and try new things,' she wrote. 'I honestly think it made me a better person being there because everyone was so lovely and welcoming, and they treat each other with such kindness. It's something everyone can learn from.'

The food was amazing. I cooked at home quite a bit but it was hard not to go down the street and eat fresh sushi, okonomiyaki (savoury pancakes made of cabbage) and okinawan (purple potatoes, which are served steamed and have a slightly sweet, creamy texture, like having dessert). Eating was an experience, from the restaurants that served tiny plates that changed every day to barbecue places that gave you the ingredients so you could cook the meal yourself. It was like a wonderland from which you always walked away feeling full, but never sluggish.

At times it was amusing to notice our differences, for instance sun tanning. Caitlin and I got some very strange looks when we lay in the sun in the car park of the apartment building, not because of where we were lying but because we wanted tans. Even in the humid conditions of a Japanese summer, our Sendai team-mates would wear long sleeves and layers of sunscreen. They told us that in Japan how white you are is an indication of your wealth and success. Tanned skin suggests you are poor and work outdoors, in the fields.

There were more surprises when we arrived for training at the club's ground, Yurtec Stadium. Our Japanese team-mates arrived an hour or so beforehand to clean the change rooms and even wipe down the balls before training. It was spotless by the time we arrived. Afterwards, they often stayed behind for extra practice and to clean up after themselves, which is even more remarkable when they were semi-professional and had other jobs to go to during the day. It was not done to impress us as guests, but the way they always behaved—with respect—and fitted neatly into the team's pledge 'to work hard and inspire', as well as their slogan 'Shoot for the Stars'.

Playing in Japan was always going to be a challenge for me and Caitlin. There were obvious language barriers, although we had a translator at training and sometimes it was clear our team-mates understood more English than they let on. For a while Caitlin and I struggled but it's funny how instinct takes over after a while and you know where players are on the field and where you are supposed to be without great conversations.

Still, we did learn a few basic, necessary words like left (*hidari*) and right (*migi*) and press (*puresu*) as in to press forward.

I was in awe of the Japanese short-passing skills and it had often been our undoing when the Matildas played against their national team. The way they played 'like shadows' forced us to play an awkward 'man-up' tactic to try to counter and disrupt their tactics.

So here was a chance to learn from them and improve my own skill set. It was the opportunity that I missed in Kansas three years before, where I desperately wanted to pit myself against American stars and become a better player but was largely ignored. But here in Sendai, Caitlin and I were welcomed into the fold and admired for our own styles and abilities.

At first our efforts during their intricate drills must have seemed almost clumsy, particularly in an exercise called circle ball in which two girls in the middle have to try to get the ball from the girls forming a circle around them. I felt like a headless chook running around, unable to keep up with their deft one-touch passing. Left foot, right foot—it didn't matter.

There was also a warm-up juggling exercise where you had to take two touches and pass. At first, Caitlin and I couldn't work out how they were doing this with such precision but practice is what it's all about and for the first time since I was a kid learning tricks for lolly prizes at Mount Gravatt, I would go home afterwards and practise and practise.

Caitlin and I would team up in training, fearing we might embarrass ourselves, but in the end we realised that we came here to get better which meant we had to get out of our comfort zones. It worked; we both improved, not only in terms of anticipation and timing of interception but in our passing skills.

I had wondered how my own, more aggressive style of play would fit into their team. Would I have to temper my defensive enthusiasm and attacking desire and pass rather than shoot from outside the box? The answer was no, as my team-mates and even the coach not only enjoyed but were excited by my defensive efforts and tackling, dubbing me *Macho Mini.*

Caitlin and I knew each other's games and we linked up well on the field where her speed meant she scored goals and was a big factor in our season where we finished a creditable fourth.

I was pretty happy with my form overall, once getting Most Valuable Player for a game. My prize was a ten-kilogram bag of rice.

For all the Japanese players' finesse, Caitlin and I were faster, fitter and stronger simply because that's the way we train and play. The gym at the club was virtually empty because none of them did strength training beyond stretching and some core work. I never saw any of them lift a weight, which brings me to another point—negotiating our tattoos.

The Japanese did not like tattoos on women because they are associated with criminal gangs, so we were banned from entering gyms unless we could cover our tattoos up with tape. Sadly, that was almost impossible if we wanted to go to an *onsen*, one of the amazing natural hot spring baths, because I simply have too many tattoos to cover up, including one I had done while I was in Japan—a Koi fish on my hip alongside maps of Australia and Japan.

My tattoos are my storyline: a map of my life and experiences—good and bad—that have made up my journey so far.

As usual, family came first, even when it came to my body artwork. It was just after my eighteenth birthday when I had the words *Mum* and *Dad* inked on either wrist in a way that what I see is the reverse, which rather cleverly reads *I love*. I have a design for my sister Amanda on my ribs—*AJG Alis volat propriis*—which is Latin for 'she flies by her own wings'; an eternity sign with all my brothers' names and a puzzle piece especially for Dylan, because he was the last piece of the family jigsaw.

There is a tree along my right forearm whose branches contain the names of my nieces and nephews, so it grows with each birth in the family. Clara and I are represented by twin poppies, Harper's foot is on my ankle, and even my dogs Simba and Rio are remembered with little pawprints.

I also have tattoos to tell the story of my career as a footballer, including a clock on my left side with the hands pointing to 7 and 11 o'clock to indicate the date (11 July) that I debuted for the Matildas. On my back I have wings which I had done during a particularly difficult time to remind myself that I could keep on flying, as well as the number 23 because 2023 was a good year for me, both professionally and personally. Wrapped around my thigh are the words *We don't see things as they are, we see things as we are* to describe the way I was feeling about the world and myself when I was in Norway in 2019.

Around the same time I also had a second reminder inked behind my left ear—*I am the hero of this story*—which is a reminder that I am responsible for the decisions in my life. So make them wisely.

The freshness of my experience in Japan was a blessing for many hidden reasons. In the months leading up to the move I had begun to question my long-term relationship with my partner, who was also a football player.

We'd spent close to five years together but the relationship had waned, partly because we were at different stages in our careers. I was young and on the way up and she was a bit older, had had a long and successful career and was winding down to retirement from the game. It meant that we were apart for long periods of time, which puts pressure on any relationship.

She had been the girl for me and we had even discussed my desire for children but the long-distance phone calls had become an ever-lengthening distance between us and we had nothing to say to each other anymore. I felt as if I wasn't good enough and couldn't give her what she wanted and needed in the relationship. There was no anger, just sadness.

Mynavi Sendai was a welcome distraction but the situation began to wear me down as the season progressed. I was playing virtually every game and training hard, but when I was alone in the apartment at night, it was inevitable that my thoughts would turn to home and family and lovers.

I had to make a decision—to accept the way things were and relax or to end it and move on. It sounds harsh but I find it hard to deal with things I can't control, at least to some degree, so I ended it with a phone call one night. It took her by surprise and we both ended up crying. My wounds, self-inflicted as they were, would remain open and raw for some time.

There were two other negatives bouncing around my head. The first was the penalty kick in Rio. It was almost a year earlier by then but I could not shake it and probably never will. *What if, what if, what if.* It could have been a turning point for Australian women's football if we'd made the semi-final, let alone if we had got to the final and beyond.

But it stopped right there when I missed. I did the best I could in the moment but had I practised enough? Was I good enough? The thoughts would not stop.

The other issue was far more personal. My brother Joel was an ice addict.

It's hard to talk about this publicly but he and I both agree that it's an important part of telling my story so people understand what impact drugs can have on a family and how elite athletes deal with the same issues as everyone else.

Joel's story was a classic situation in which he began with something relatively innocent, like alcohol and marijuana, and then, as other aspects of his life went astray he got caught up with the wrong crowd and began to take more and more risks. By the age of eighteen he was hanging around with what we called 'the shopping mall gangsters'. He became bored and angry about life and spent less and less time at home.

There was one incident when he and his mates were drinking on the roof of a supermarket when the police arrived. Everyone scattered but, instead of running downstairs like the others, Joel leaped off the roof and fell two storeys, snapping his leg in half.

Mum went to the hospital to see him and Joel, with his leg in a cast from hip to toe, asked where his friends were. 'They've all gone,' she replied. 'You're all alone'.

But the experience didn't stop him from using drugs. Instead, they began to play a more prominent role in his life—a way of losing himself rather than facing life's difficult decisions.

It was around this time that I began playing professionally, and spending a lot of time in Melbourne and Adelaide, so I wasn't around to see what was happening to Joel. I'm not even sure what could have been done because, like all people who use drugs, he hid his habits so we were unaware of how bad things were becoming.

I was lucky in the sense that I had a passion and a goal that drove me down a pathway that was too narrow to accommodate a drugs lifestyle. I feared at one stage that my success had helped make life difficult for Joel. We are only a year apart and it would have been understandable for him to feel judged for not being as successful as me.

His descent became evident soon after I got back from Ottawa in 2012, when he was convicted of wilful damage at a bowls club. Police had been called to an out-of-control birthday party where Joel was at the centre of the scuffle, using line markers pulled from the bowling green as weapons.

He fled the scene and was found soon afterwards, shirtless by the side of the road and clearly affected by alcohol, drugs or both: 'I'm the one you're looking for,' he told them.

By the time the charges reached court he had shown remorse and paid the club for the broken markers. He insisted he was trying to defend himself and had ended up in hospital that night after 'taking a flogging'. Despite his contriteness, the magistrate fined him $400 and recorded a conviction, which is a scar for life.

We were all shocked, a mix of concern and anger about what was happening. We felt powerless to do anything about it. Something was desperately wrong but, despite his public shame, Joel remained caught in the grip of the drug crystal meth, which is rampant across many Australian cities. It would be some years before anything would change.

I think it was one of the reasons that I felt so compassionate about the homeless men and women I met in Ottawa. It was clear that most of them were, or had been, affected by drugs, whether it was ice or alcohol. It's easy to get angry at the person for seemingly being so foolish and weak but that is never the whole story.

The turning point for our family was 2016 when Joel arrived for the family Christmas dinner. As he walked in, one of my uncles was telling a story about a black dog and a bicycle and Joel, in his drug haze, thought we were all talking about him behind his back and we were telling him to kill himself.

He responded angrily and began shouting at my uncle, who couldn't understand what was going on. Things got very loud before Joel backed off and apologised, but then it happened again and again. Our Christmas was ruined.

Things were still in a mess when I left for Japan as Joel resisted all our attempts to convince him to seek help. Mum and Dad were constantly worried about where he was and what he was doing, fearing the worst as it became clearer just how bad his habit had become. I couldn't do anything, except hope and be available if there was a need, so Japan was a kind of distraction.

In July I got a phone call from Mum to tell me that Joel had finally agreed to go into a rehab facility and get some help. It was a traumatic situation but I felt relief, particularly when I was later told that Dad had gone around to the house where Joel lived on and off, and found him in the backyard about to hang himself.

He had reached rock bottom and written a note about his desperation to find a way out of the grip of the drugs that were wrecking his life.

He entered a facility in Gympie, an hour or so north of Brisbane, where he initially had no contact with the outside world.

All I could do was hold my breath and hope.

CHAPTER FIFTEEN

Jade and Joel

If there is one thing that unifies the Matildas it's coffee. Whenever we travel to train and play, the first thing we do is search the town or city where we're staying to find the cafe of choice. The search gets quite competitive, actually, and it is a badge of honour to be the one who finds the best brew.

This was especially so in July 2017 when we all came together to play in the inaugural Tournament of Nations, the brainchild of the US Soccer Federation to give its national team a hit-out against rival nations in years when there are no Olympics or World Cup.

The US, Japan, Brazil and Australia—all ranked in the top eight sides in the world—would face off in a series of round-robin matches played across three US cities. It copied the format of the SheBelieves Cup staged the year before and again featuring the US, this time against three leading European teams: Germany, England and France.

The timing was perfect for us because a lot of the squad were already in America playing for various clubs in the National Women's Soccer League. Sam Kerr was running amok for Sky Blue, Lydia Williams at Houston, Steph Catley and Alanna Kennedy at Orlando Pride, and Ashleigh Sykes and Hayley Raso at Portland.

Caitlin and I almost didn't make it to the tournament as Mynavi Sendai tried to stop us competing so we could play for the team in a finals match that clashed with the Matildas games. I begged and eventually they relented so we arrived in Seattle, where the first match would be played, on the same flight as the Japanese national team, a squad that included three of our Mynavi Sendai team-mates, Emi Nakajima, Miho Manya and Nana Ichise. We all posed for a photo on arrival, which I posted on Instagram—team-mates one day, enemies the next—before going into our respective camps.

As it turned out, Seattle is a famous American coffee town where beans have been pan-roasted since the late nineteenth century. The cobblestone streets around the Pike Place Market near the waterfront were teeming with cafes like Storyville Coffee and Le Panier, and Starbucks opened its first store here using locally grown beans.

The environment inside team camps is integral to your performance on the pitch and coffee seemed to be our team glue, whether we were sitting out in the sunshine at a cafe or sending a couple of players off in an Uber to fetch orders. The main challenge was to find a barista who knew how to make an Aussie flat white. Quite often we were met with bemused faces, so a latte became the acceptable alternative.

Cards was another way to bond as we'd play games in the afternoons as we rested between training sessions. A game called Shithead was our favourite (the name is apparently a mistranslation of a Swedish word *skitgubbe*, which means grubby old man). No money ever changed hands but, as usual, everything was competitive. I can't stand losing at anything.

But we were in America to do business. Although the tournament was billed as a 'friendly', none of us was taking the event as anything other than a serious hit-out, and our respective records at major international tournaments showed the challenge we faced.

The Matildas had never made it past the quarter-finals at either the World Cup or the Olympics, whereas Brazil had finished runner-up at both tournaments; Japan had won the 2011 World Cup and were finalists at the 2012 Olympics while the US were three-time World Cup champions and four-time Olympic champions.

But we had been on a steady rise since Staj took over the reins three years before, and he saw this as an opportunity to get the Matildas firmly on the stage as genuine contenders in major tournaments ahead of the 2019 World Cup in France.

I was not in a good place mentally. Apart from my own sense of failure after Brazil, I was worried about Joel. He was now in rehab but it was hard not to be concerned as the days passed and there was no word on his progress. I had also begun to realise just how serious his problem had been, and that had sent ripples through my family, which prided itself on taking care of one another. When I look back at vision of myself playing during the tournament I can see the signs of the silent struggle in my eyes and my body language.

The Matildas hadn't beaten the US in twenty-six meetings between the teams; our best result being a couple of draws. This was our chance, in front of 16,000 people at CenturyLink Field (now Lumen Field) in Seattle, particularly as we matched up well physically against the powerful American team.

We began as we meant to play, pressing forward aggressively and taking the challenge directly to the reigning world champions. The action was fast and willing, the crowd boisterous and the ESPN television commentators complimentary, except for their observations about me.

'There is Katrina Gorry. She is only four feet eight inches tall.'

Pardon me, but I'm five foot one inches tall on the old scale, and why does it make any difference when I am a midfielder playing her fifty-third international? I thought those sorts of comments had vanished after my junior days.

Despite my darkening mood I was playing quite well, hitting a low, long-range effort that was saved by the keeper and then almost sending Lisa De Vanna through late in the first half before the offside flag went up.

The US had their own chances and it was only through Lydia Williams' efforts in goal that we weren't behind at half-time, as she blocked veteran Megan Rapinoe with a one-handed effort at the near post and then made two great saves to deny World Player of the Year Carli Lloyd.

We started strongly in the second half and our moment arrived with twenty minutes to go when the USA failed to clear their defence lines. Emily van Egmond pounced on a contested ball on the edge of the area and it fell clear to Tameka Butt who, under pressure, lashed a shot across American goalkeeper Alyssa Naeher and into the net.

The convergence of team-mates after the goal was a leaping, joyous crush of gold shirts as we realised that we were on the verge of a famous win and a watershed moment for Australian women's football.

But it wasn't that easy as the USA regrouped, unwilling to give up their perfect record against us. I had a heart-stopping moment just before full-time when I challenged Megan Rapinoe and was shown a yellow card, but the resulting free kick went wide and high, and we were able to hold firm in the four minutes of extra time.

The final whistle set off another frenzy of celebrations as we ran crazily around the field, which showed just how much the win meant to us. It felt like we had just won the World Cup as we did a lap of honour to an appreciative crowd.

'The Matildas have waltzed into history,' the ESPN commentator observed with a chuckle at his Aussie cultural reference. 'Their first ever victory over the United States. Congratulations to them.'

Japan, who had drawn 1–1 with Brazil in the first round, was our next challenge. Although we fell behind early on, we showed our rising confidence against the Asian champions by striking back in the tenth minute when Sam Kerr scored from close range and then added a second goal four minutes later with a bullet from just outside the box.

Sam made it 3–1 just two minutes before half-time, this time with a solo effort when she nodded the ball over a defender on the halfway line then dribbled under pressure to shoot into the feet of the goalkeeper who blocked the shot. Sam stayed on her feet and picked off the rebound to score before running off towards the sideline to perform a backflip in celebration. A second-half penalty taken by Emily van Egmond gave us a 4–2 result.

Caitlin Foord revealed later that Sam had predicted her hat-trick in an Instagram message before the match. The message thread began with a question from Caitlin to the captain: 'Are you going to score today?'

'Yeh,' Sam responded, '3 haha!'

After the game, Caitlin approached Sam. 'No words, freak!'

Staj sent me out to represent the team at the post-match media conference: 'I thought we played pretty well in patches,' I said without really smiling. 'We dominated the game for the most part, Sammy scored a hat-trick and, yeah, it was a good day at the office.'

A good day at the office? Talk about an understatement to explain our best ever win over Japan. When I watch the video clip now I can see the lacklustre look in my eyes and flat body language, which echoed how I felt at the time. I was physically fit and eager to participate but off the pitch I couldn't shake the sense of an approaching darkness.

The victory over Japan meant we just needed a draw in the last game against Brazil to win the entire tournament. The South Americans had lost in a remarkable game against the USA. Brazil had led 3–1 with ten minutes to go before the Americans scored three goals in the last nine minutes to win 4–3.

We ran onto the ground at Carson, about 20 kilometres from downtown Los Angeles, wearing black armbands in respect of veteran commentator Les Murray who had died a few days before the match. It was Staj's idea. There was a great deal of respect for Les, known as Mr Football, who helped promote the game in Australia from its infancy back in the 1970s.

The match didn't start well for us, falling behind within two minutes when we conceded a free kick and Camila scored from the top of the box. But it wasn't long before we equalised when Sam Kerr was brought down in the box. Lisa De Vanna's resulting penalty was saved but the goalkeeper could only parry the ball away and Lisa pounced on the rebound and scored. The goal made Lisa the Matildas' leading goal-scorer of all time, with forty-two, although Sam Kerr has since blasted past that figure.

We were on a roll as first Caitlin Foord and then Lisa scored after assists from Sam to make it 3–1. Then it was my turn, using my turn of pace to beat a couple of defenders inside the box before angling the ball across the keeper. I felt good about the goal but, despite media assertions to the contrary, it did not make up for my penalty miss in Rio de Janeiro—not even close.

We couldn't quite believe we were up 4–1 during the break and emerged from the change rooms with the only tactic that seemed to make sense in the circumstance—to score again, which we did.

Caitlin made it five when she latched onto a through-ball from Tameka and got around the keeper, and then Sam bustled through the defence to tap it home for a memorable 6–1 result, Brazil's biggest defeat in almost two decades.

Staj was ecstatic as he faced the media: 'To get the monkey off our back adds to our self-belief. Japan, we've beaten at their home. America, we've beaten at their home, and they're the last two World Cup finalists. We had a draw against Germany at the Olympics last year and they ended up winning the gold medal. We've shown we can beat the best teams in the world on their home turf and the challenge is now for us to do it for a few games in a row at a major tournament to win the thing.'

I didn't return to Japan immediately, instead flying home to Queensland for a couple of days for two personal and very different reasons. The first was Jade and Jenna's wedding, where I was a bridesmaid and where a dress, ordered from afar, was waiting for me.

But would I get there in time? I left the ground immediately after the game against Brazil and raced to Los Angeles Airport for an overnight flight to Australia. I was hoping to reach the Sunshine Coast in the early morning of the ceremony but soon hit complications, beginning with a four-hour delay at LAX.

I was becoming increasingly worried, wondering whether I should alert Jade to the problem or leave her alone and hope for the best. In the end, I chose the latter; there was nothing either of us could do about it anyway and there was no need to worry her.

Jade was not just my best friend but family and I wanted to be there for her, no matter where I was playing in the world. Jade remembers that I arrived barely an hour before the ceremony, jet-lagged with a brain like mush and ill-prepared to give a speech that I cannot remember.

What I do recall is standing on a balcony overlooking the ocean and hugging Jade, so happy to be there with her at such an important moment in her life and proud to be her best friend. Football is a passing thrill and achievement but friendship and family are an enduring love.

The second reason I returned home was so that I could visit Joel in rehab. It was Sunday afternoon and Mum and I drove north to Gympie, which is about an hour north of the Sunshine Coast where the wedding had been held the previous day.

It was an emotional reunion that day. The change in my brother was stark. Instead of the dark, evasive and angry young man who ranted and railed at the Christmas dinner, he was calmer and contrite, so sorry about his actions and their impact on the family. But he was still fragile and a long way from good health.

Detox had been a nightmare but he felt he was through the worst. He had been in there for a month and had another two months to go, but the situation had been complicated because a friend of his inside the clinic had committed suicide.

It highlighted to me just how little I had understood the impact drugs could have on people, and how immensely difficult it is to free yourself. You don't realise how hard it is until you see someone you love go through the ordeal. The stories he told us that day were frightening.

I left with the words of an older coach of mine ringing in my ears. She had been a long-time police officer and I had spoken to her often about Joel and what we could do to help him. Her reply was chilling: there was really nothing we could do; Joel had to do it himself and, even if he went to rehab, only a small percentage of people fully recover. All I could do was hope that my brother would be among that minority.

CHAPTER SIXTEEN

The Perils of Expectation

At the beginning of 2018, the Matildas were as close to the top of the football world as we had ever been—ranked fourth behind the USA, Germany and England and ahead of rivals like Japan, Brazil and Sweden.

The Matildas camp was buzzing about what lay ahead with the World Cup less than two years away. We were on a winning streak, returning from our triumph in America at the Tournament of Nations to what the media described as 'a hero's welcome', which seemed a little over the top except that our next two matches, in September against Brazil, produced two record crowds—15,089 in Penrith and 16,829 in Newcastle.

We had played in front of bigger crowds overseas, but not here in Australia. You could feel the excitement that our performances were generating and we responded, dominating possession in the two hard-fought games during which we fired off thirty-five shots to fifteen to win 2–1 and 3–2 respectively. 'Matildas dazzle', the headlines read. We were *ambassadors* and *a wonderful team*. Australia was proud of women's sport.

Lisa De Vanna, who opened the scoring, summed up our feelings after the first game: 'I've been in the team for fifteen years and I've never been in a stadium where there have been fifteen thousand fans shouting for the Matildas. I was holding back the tears during the national anthem.'

When the team won the public vote as the team of the year at the AIS awards, and Sam Kerr and Staj were voted ABC Sports Personality of the Year and Coach of the Year, we knew something magical was happening. Women's football had risen above the major sports off the back of a tournament described as 'friendly'.

But that's where danger also lay. The mood at our training camps was buoyant, Staj even allowing a journalist inside to do a background piece on the team and our success. I remember the article well, partly because it featured my relationship with my roomie Michelle Heyman as an example of the team's strong bonds.

Staj summed it up well: 'We are a family. There are tight bonds here. People can come here and they have fun, the players enjoy coming to camp and spending time together. When you come to a place with that sense of being yourself, being authentic and not pretending, ultimately that leads to you feeling the pressure of performing but not the pressure of being someone you're not. They're not easy periods leading into major tournaments but certainly in that process we solidified our playing style and that gave the players a lot of confidence in themselves and the team. When you have that confidence in your team-mates and belief that we can achieve things together, that strengthens the bonds we already have.'

I'd been a bit vocal myself in the media, especially after we had two good wins over China the previous November. The matches were building blocks for the next couple of years, I said in an ABC interview after our 3–0 victory in Geelong.

'Our focus is going to be on the Algarve Cup and seeing what we can do there. We played pretty well last year so hopefully we'll expect to bring home silverware. Leading into the Asian Cup, we're probably favourites in Asia at the moment and we've instilled a bit of fear—people are scared of us now—so I think that's going to be pretty exciting leading into the Asian Cup and we've got to keep on building.'

So there it was. The word *expect*, thrown in with the added notion that we were *feared*. Looking back, it's pretty clear that we were setting ourselves up for a fall. It was one thing to be confident, but *aiming* to win would have been more realistic than *expecting* to triumph, just as being *respected* would have been better than *feared*.

For once, we were the highest-ranked team at the tournament, ahead of Canada (5) and the Netherlands (7).

We were drawn in Pool A with China (9), Norway (14) and the hosts Portugal which, at 38, was the lowest-ranked team in the tournament.

But, as we would learn, rankings mean little in a tournament situation, particularly as we were without six first-team players who were out through injury. Then came the weather.

We started well enough and all seemed to be on target when we built a 3–1 first-half lead over Norway in very windy conditions. Even though they had scored first, Clare Polkinghorne had struck back within two minutes with a great header from a corner kick. Chloe Logarzo volleyed home ten minutes later, followed soon afterwards when Sam Kerr scored for a record seventh match in a row.

But that's where things stopped. Norway scored a few minutes after the restart as we struggled in the blustery and rainy conditions, then Elise Hove Thorsnes, who had already scored in the first half for Norway, struck again from the penalty spot and we had thrown away a two-goal lead.

A draw seemed likely until Larissa Crummer poked the ball into the net after a goalmouth scrimmage with what would be the last kick of the game to give us a hard-fought 4–3 win. It was our eighth win in a row and Staj insisted he was happy, given the distance we had to travel, the loss of players and the conditions.

'I'm proud of how we managed to stay in the game,' he told the media. 'We managed to play our way out and we stayed true to our positive selves.'

There was every reason to be positive in our next game against Portugal, just two days later. Not only did we expect to win, but we wanted to do so convincingly to celebrate Clare Polkinghorne's hundredth game. I posed with her and Michelle Heyman in the change rooms before the match, dressed in a Matildas jersey with a big yellow 100 emblazoned on the front and an Australian flag on the wall in the background. I stuck it on Instagram with this message:

> No words can sum up the player and person you are @polks89. You are something special.

Clare was given the captaincy for the game but our performance fell well short of the hype and we struggled to a 0–0 draw. We were willing enough but the pitch was boggy, which probably accounted for the disjointed performance and few scoring opportunities. We also should have had a penalty early in the game when Chloe was brought down inside the box, only for the referee to change her mind and award a free kick outside the box.

We dominated the second half but could not make the breakthrough as our injury list grew. Emily Condon went off with an ankle injury and I got a bad knock late in the game.

Still, we were on top of the Pool A table with the last match to go, against the Chinese whom we needed to not only beat but win by several goals to ensure we made the final at the expense of the other pool winners.

We had beaten the Chinese comfortably a few months before, scoring eight goals, but we were lucky not to be behind at half-time as China had several chances go begging and we struggled midfield to get anything going.

Thankfully things turned around after the break and in the fifty-first minute Alanna Kennedy put a nice cross into the box where Chloe looped a header over the keeper's head. But a 1–0 win was not good enough and we continued to press without luck until a late goal by Sam made it 2–0.

It was not enough as our goal difference fell short of Spain and the Netherlands who would meet in the final. Instead, we would meet Portugal again for the bronze medal and a chance to redeem ourselves.

Sam Kerr and I both started on the bench for the match as Staj rotated the squad with an eye on the upcoming World Cup qualifiers in Jordan. The weather was again shitty, windy and rainy when it should have been calm and pleasant. It was so bad that the final between Spain and the Netherlands, scheduled to start a few hours after our match, was abandoned, forcing a strange dual-winner end to the tournament.

The conditions made it difficult to play with any confidence and, apart from a free kick by Elise Kellond-Knight which rattled the post, nothing much happened until a defensive error allowed Portugal in and they took the lead. Thankfully, Caitlin Cooper, who had been involved in a mix-up with Lydia Williams which allowed the Portuguese goal, made amends right on half-time with a back post header that brought us back level.

We were playing below par and Portugal were playing above themselves and they continued to do so early in the second half, peppering our goal. After several chances, Vanessa Malho put one past Lydia from outside the box to give them the lead once again.

Sam and I were both brought into the game midway through the half and we looked to have equalised when she was brought down in the box. But Portugal's young keeper, eighteen-year-old Ines Pereira, saved Emily van Egmond's kick and Portugal held on for their biggest victory, and our shame.

Fourth place was beginning to suck.

There was a short turnaround between the Algarve Cup and the Asian Cup in Jordan, which would, as usual, decide the Asian participants in the World Cup in 2019. There was enough time to head home for a few weeks and play a friendly against Thailand, in Perth, the day before both teams flew to Jordan.

The 5–0 result was comforting and showed our attacking potential, which South Korea, our first opponents, did their best to starve by setting their defensive lines deep and hoping to sneak a goal with a counter-attack rather than take the match up to us.

The latter scenario did not happen—I don't think Lydia Williams even touched the ball during the game—but the tactic worked in the sense that we only had one decent shot on goal, and that was through Kyah Simon when she came on late. The match finished 0–0.

Suddenly our next match against Vietnam became important, not because we needed to win—that was almost a given—but we had to win by more goals than Japan who had thrashed them 4–0.

We achieved our objective with an 8–0 drubbing. We were six goals up early in the second half when I came on as a substitute and my only disappointment was that I seemed to be the only one who didn't score.

South Korea was at it again in the other match, drawing 0–0 with Japan, which meant that we could draw against the Japanese and still top the group pool, given our scoring frenzy against Vietnam.

But a draw against our old nemesis Japan was not a certainty and a loss would place us in a lottery for the fifth, and last, spot in the World Cup. We dominated possession in the first half but lacked penetration against a tight and well-managed Japanese team.

Our misses in front of goal looked to have cost us midway through the second half when Japan made a rare sortie forward and midfielder Mizuho Sakaguchi scored. We were in trouble until Sam Kerr found a way when, with four minutes on the clock, she latched onto a low cross and turned it into the net from a sharp angle.

We had finished on top of the group and drew Thailand in a semi-final, a match we expected to win given their ranking of 30 and the fact that we had just thrashed them 5–0 earlier in Perth.

But a semi-final is different from a friendly and Thailand took the game right up to us that day. We scored first via an own goal by a Thai defender but then a series of defensive blunders allowed Thailand to score twice and lead with a few minutes to go. A shock defeat loomed until injury time when Alanna Kennedy nodded in a corner kick to level the scores. It would come down to penalty kicks after we wasted several opportunities.

Our goalkeeper Mackenzie Arnold then saved three consecutive Thai penalties and Sam Kerr sealed our berth in the final.

There was a sense of relief that, despite some questionable performances, we had qualified for the World Cup. But could we overturn recent history and beat Japan to win a significant piece of silverware?

For once we seemed to have the upper hand, as we clearly outplayed them in the first half, although we couldn't put the ball in the back of the net. Sam Kerr was denied twice while Steph Catley, Emily van Egmond, Tameka Butt and Lisa De Vanna missed chances before the Japanese goalkeeper Ayaka Yamashita saved Elise Kellond-Knight's penalty kick.

The second half settled down a little although we still had chances, including a long-range shot by Emily which crashed against the bar. Then the unthinkable happened: with just six minutes left, Japanese substitute Kumi Yokoyama played in behind our defence and hit a fabulous strike into the top corner.

We had lost 1–0 to Japan yet again in a final, despite being dominant in possession and firing off twenty-three shots on goal compared to Japan's five.

There was another reason for our frustrations—me. I was out of form and struggling psychologically. Being back in Brisbane before the tournament had only exacerbated the misgivings I was having about life, and it was clearly affecting my performance, as one journalist noted while summing up the Japan final:

'Not helping the Matildas' cause was Katrina Gorry's struggle to find form throughout the tournament. At her best, the playmaker creates goals with ease. But she looked off all tournament and was benched for the final—and wasn't called upon as a second-half substitute.'

It was true. I hadn't scored a goal for a dozen internationals and my position in the starting line-up was now under question as I headed off to America for their domestic season. Perhaps time away from Australia would help.

CHAPTER SEVENTEEN

The Edge of Darkness

I was twenty-five years old and standing on top of the mountain that I had so desperately wanted to climb. I was now part of a team that had the potential to be the best in the world. So why did this mountain top, with its views of potential splendour, feel like a clifftop with a crumbling edge?

I can see now that my psychological foundations were fragile. The disappointment of the penalty miss in Rio still weighed heavily on me. It was like a broken record in my head that found its way into my sleep and made me question myself again and again. Joel's drug nightmare was real and unyielding. Yes, he was in treatment and appeared to have turned the corner, but how had it ever reached this stage? Was my success partly to blame for his troubles?

I was beginning to question myself and my life. My decision to break up with my long-term girlfriend around this time had also opened a wound and I found myself pushing people away. I had a desire for sanctuary and love, the kind that a proper relationship brings, but I now found it difficult to trust. I was disappointed, especially as having children seemed further away than ever.

My football career was going well. I had just become the first Brisbane Roar player to get a multi-year contract and the club had triumphed by winning the premiership in 2017–18 with nine wins from twelve games (I only played in five because of international commitments), but I felt emotionally flat and drained. For the first time in my life I realised that football wasn't enough.

So, I was excited to take up an opportunity to play a season with the Utah Royals, even though I had misgivings about America after my experience in Kansas four years earlier. It seemed like the kind of change I needed. The Utah team was a new franchise in the National Women's Soccer League with money and excitement behind the venture. Two of my team-mates from my time in Kansas, Becky Sauerbrunn and Amy Rodriguez, had also been picked up by the club. Amy, in particular, was an inspiration to me.

The Utah head coach Laura Harvey was enthusiastic when my selection was announced: 'Katrina is a player that I have watched for a few years now. She has experience of playing in the US with FC Kansas City,' she said in a club press release. 'Since she was here, she has gone away and developed her game further, and now together we felt it was the right time for her to come back to the league. Katrina has proven she can play anywhere in the world and I'm excited to get her back to the NWSL.'

When I first arrived at the club I felt rejuvenated. The Matildas may have just lost the Asian Cup final again, but we had achieved the most important aspect of the campaign: to qualify for the World Cup. I now had six months where I could leave my problems back in Brisbane and concentrate on a new American experience.

Salt Lake City is amazing culturally and geographically. Built by Mormon settlers on the banks of the Great Salt Lake, it has a backdrop of mountains filled with hiking trails, where I would often find myself on weekends. The city was made for me culturally, with a strong LGBTQI community, a long-standing annual Pride march and, while I was there, an openly lesbian mayor.

'A really funky city,' was how I described it in a promotional interview midway through the season. 'I wasn't sure what to expect when I arrived but it's one of the most incredible clubs I've played with.'

I wasn't being totally truthful, at least about the way I was feeling about the season. I hadn't left my problems at home at all; instead I had packed them inside my head and brought them with me. And, unlike a suitcase, you can't unpack your head, store it in a wardrobe and forget about it until you're ready to leave.

I found myself moving away from the football crowd, towards a new group of friends I'd met one day in a cafe. I tried dating on an app, not to find a partner but simply to fill my cup in another way. I was full of questions about the game and my future. Did I want to play anymore? And if I didn't, then what was I going to do with my life?

I had spoken to a psychologist a couple of times in Brisbane before I left, and seemed to be addressing things, but being away from home with no support was highlighting my misgivings. I hated being away from my family and only seeing them on a computer screen a couple of times a week. If I was at home and had had a crappy day, I would jump in the car and drive over to Dad and Michelle's house to spend a few hours with Dylan, simply because he makes me feel better about the world.

In my growing sense of despair I needed to grab hold of something that made me feel as if I had some sort of control over my life. I chose food. What had begun in Tokyo with Mynavi Sendai as calorie counting was about to spiral out of control. I began a hideous cycle of starving myself to binge-eating and back again.

There were days that I wouldn't eat anything other than a protein shake and then, when my body screamed out for something, I would order takeaway or stand at the fridge door and eat whatever was in there. If I ate toast and a bowl of cereal for breakfast I'd reach for the packet and fill another bowl, and then another, thinking I may as well have another one because I'm going to feel like crap anyway.

To compound the problem, I would begin most days with an F45 class, a high-octane workout lasting forty-five minutes, at the local gym, after which I would often stay for a hot yoga class before going to football training that afternoon. It was a ridiculous schedule even for an elite young athlete. I was driving myself into the ground, physically and mentally.

It is almost impossible to describe the sensation of despair in the pit of self-loathing. I'm not even sure how I fell into it, but trying to climb out again was so exhausting that it seemed a better option to accept it and feed the psychological cravings.

If I had stopped and thought about it, I might have realised that I was following my brother Joel's path into a dangerous obsessive behaviour that could take control of my life.

Sporting injuries tend to be black and white. You can identify what is injured and how it happened, followed by surgery to fix the problem and time to heal and recuperate. It's essentially a job of mechanics, like fixing a car.

But psychological problems are not so clear. They are a series of greys that seem to arrive from nowhere and everywhere, and come and go almost as if your mind is taunting you.

Some days I enjoyed football and other days I hated every minute and couldn't wait to get away.

Some of my Utah team-mates could see what was going on but I wasn't in the right head space to open up, partly because I couldn't answer their questions. Nothing made sense to me then, particularly when my whole life had operated on a combination of instinct and logic until that point.

The one person I talked to openly was my room-mate, Norwegian player Elise Thorsnes. She recognised that my eating habits were not normal and told me that she had suffered similar bouts of trying to control her food. We had several conversations about it, which gave me some sense of relief that there was a way out of this maze, but then she got injured and went home early and I was suddenly alone.

There were days when I didn't feel as if I had the energy to get out of bed, let alone go to training, weighed down by a darkness that I didn't recognise and couldn't describe. On other days I sought solace in the mountains behind the city, taking long walks or simply sitting and reading.

I had to snap out of it, particularly as the Matildas had one more important tournament before the year's end, a year in which we played seventeen internationals. The Tournament of Nations, played in late July and early August 2018, was described as a friendly but, as defending champions, we took it very seriously.

Our first match was back in Kansas against Brazil, who were coming off a run of seven straight victories. We had started to exert a bit of dominance over them in recent games and we began well again. We were 3–0 up by half-time thanks to an own goal and two more added by Tameka and Sam. We eased off in the second half to win 3–1.

Next up was the USA, a match I would sit out on the bench, which sums up my situation at the time. We managed to get an early goal against the run of play when Lisa De Vanna made one of her typical bustling runs from defence into attack before sliding the ball to Chloe Logarzo who made no mistake and slotted it past the keeper.

For the next seventy minutes we held at bay an increasingly frustrated USA. Even though they dominated play at times they could not find a way through our tight defence. Then in the ninety-first minute the equaliser came from a disputed corner kick and we had to settle for a draw.

We faced Japan in the final game, determined for revenge after the Asian Cup final disappointment and keen to defend our crown. Instead, the first half was lacklustre and disjointed. It wasn't until Alanna Kennedy scored with a sensational free kick early in the second half that we woke up.

Sam Kerr added a second goal with ten minutes to play and the 2–0 result was not only satisfying but meant the USA had to win by the same margin against Brazil in a later game to stop us winning the tournament. Brazil scored first but the Americans were too strong and scored four times to snatch the title from our grasp. It was a disappointing result but our performances were, nonetheless, very satisfying.

After the tournament I returned briefly to Utah to see out the season with the Royals, starting on the bench for our last game against Chicago, whose line-up included Sam Kerr. There was a crowd of over 11,000 to watch the game, which we came from behind to win 2–1 (Sam scored, of course).

I had played in sixteen games for the Royals, mostly off the bench, as the team finished a creditable fifth in its first season. It came as no surprise when the club declined to renew my contract for the 2019 season.

The day before I left to return home, I climbed to a peak behind the city to watch the sunrise, capturing the moment in a photo for Instagram. I meant what I wrote in the caption:

> To all my team-mates, my club, our amazing supporters and every beautiful person I have met along the way, thank you for my incredible time here.

If I look back at my Instagram posts of that time I can see the subtle references I was making to my problems, frequently referring to being *lost* in the mountains, or posting photos of myself reading a book by a stream. I was trying to find the answers to the questions that were plaguing me. What was I doing here? What am I living for? And why does it matter?

I put on a mask of fabricated happiness whenever I spoke to my family. I couldn't bring myself to drag Mum and Dad into my problems when they had their own things to deal with. When we finally spoke about things later it was clear that they had sensed there was something wrong but had found it difficult to ask me about it.

I would implore anyone reading this book who finds themselves with questions and doubts to reach out to someone. Don't even hesitate to do it. We are not burdens to our friends and families, and if the boot was on the other foot then I would have wanted to know and help. It's the delay in talking that creates the burden.

It's hard to say it, but there were times during that period when I didn't really want to live anymore. It wasn't just football; everything felt so dark and I couldn't see a way out. The only way out was not being here anymore. Thankfully, my thoughts scared me enough to make me realise that I needed help.

CHAPTER EIGHTEEN

It's Okay Not To Be Okay

I was desperate to get home to Brisbane, burrow back into the sanctuary of the family fold for a while and hit a reset button. 'I feel whole again', I wrote when I was home, alongside a picture of my two dogs. They had been cared for by my sister, Amanda, who squealed with delight and leaped into my arms when I turned up at her house unannounced.

Not only was Joel clean and out of rehab but he had become a father when his daughter Amira-Lee came along a few weeks after I returned. My world was looking much better.

I was also keen to start talking to the psychologist more seriously. I had largely dismissed her suggestions when she first contacted me, prompted by team-mate Michelle Heyman's concerns about my well-being (more about that later). It wasn't because the concerns weren't valid—I knew

I needed help—but because I feared that word would get back to the team management and put my selection under threat.

It was a terrible situation when I think back on it. My reluctance to talk openly was fuelled by the messaging I'd received that as professional athletes we had to suppress anything private that might interfere with our performance.

I needed to take what the psychologist was telling me more seriously if I was going to change, and now that she was not working directly for the national team, I felt that there was no threat to my privacy.

In a way, it was like committing to training to be physically fit for a football season, only this was about understanding and managing the off-field pressures and making my brain healthy.

I began to speak out publicly about mental health, participating in a walk for mental health. I wasn't yet ready to reveal my own struggles but raised the issue on my social media feed, writing: 'Are you okay? A simple question that so many of us forget to ask.'

I opted out of a Matildas two-match Europe tour in October (they lost 2–0 to France and drew 1–1 with England) and rejoined the squad in November for two friendlies against Chile. We lost the first match 2–3 in a shock defeat but came back to win 5–0 in the second. Both matches—played in Penrith and Newcastle—were in front of 11,000-plus fans. Our popularity was continuing to grow.

But it was in Brisbane, playing with the Roar, where I would find some of the answers to my questions about the future, although not before two more setbacks. It's strange how sometimes a negative can turn out to be a blessing.

The first occurred in mid-December in a match against Melbourne. Brisbane had led comfortably 3–1 with barely ten minutes left in the game when I made a crude tackle and earned a yellow card. The problem was that I had received another yellow earlier in the match for a similar incident, so I was shown the red card and sent off just as the match was heating up, with another three goals scored in the dying minutes. Thankfully we held on for a 4–3 win.

Then, at training on Christmas Eve, as we prepared for a match against Canberra a few days later, I lunged for the ball and landed awkwardly on my left ankle under my body. I heard a pop and knew something had happened, but the physio said it looked okay and suggested strapping it up.

A few days later I could barely walk, let alone run, but because it was Christmas, it was another week before I could get a scan which confirmed that I had ruptured the syndesmosis, the point above the ankle where the tibia and fibula meet, and I needed surgery. I flew to Adelaide the next day, the only place I could get seen straight away. Michelle Heyman happened to be there and brought me food and sat with me.

My Roar season was over and I was looking at two months in a surgical boot before I could hope to resume training.

Not only had my season ended but it placed a question mark on my place in the national team for the World Cup, held in France in June.

I had never faced serious injury before, somehow avoiding anything more than a corked thigh through more than a decade of playing at an elite level, but my instinctive response surprised me. I didn't mope, as I might have, but decided that if I couldn't play then I was going to be as big a support as I could for my team-mates, particularly the young ones. Sitting on the sidelines was suddenly not so bad because I could watch others develop.

Mackenzie Arnold, our goalkeeper, noticed it when asked about the impact of my injury on the team: 'She's been really good around the team, although it's upsetting for her. She could be a real negative on the team but she hasn't been. She's been coming to every training and getting around the girls and still has a smile on her face, so it's really nice for her to do that for us.'

'A couple of tough months ahead but the reward at the end is even bigger,' I wrote on Instagram alongside a photo of me on my crutches dressed in a Roar uniform with a rather sad-looking Rio at my feet. The post got over 3000 likes from fans who were responding more and more to our social media.

As I would discover, the forced break away from the game ended up having a positive influence because it gave me the opportunity to step back and reflect on what had happened over the previous eighteen months. It also helped me to fall in love with the game all over again.

—

Everything had changed inside the Matildas when I returned to the team in late March, most noticeably that Alen Stajcic had been sacked. The news had shocked many and the official reasons would remain a mystery other than a survey cited by the FFA which concluded that Staj had overseen what they called a 'dysfunctional' and 'toxic' culture.

It was a strange time, for me personally and for the team. I was struggling to feel as if I belonged and, from a team's perspective, I knew that a lot of the girls weren't happy. Things had been pretty peachy when Staj was appointed. We had some great success and we'd risen quickly in the world rankings, but now, almost five years later, things had started to plateau and we weren't doing as well as we had hoped.

Maybe it was the stress of the job and the expectations of success, but the team environment had changed. It was now much more heightened and on edge, and the girls weren't feeling very comfortable. The way people were spoken to was different—harsher—which meant that much of the joy had disappeared. There was a sense that something needed to change and then the Professional Footballers' Association got involved and things happened very quickly.

Staj had been a fantastic coach for the Matildas. Yes, he demanded high performance, rarely seemed satisfied and had some dubious views about nutrition and weight loss, but he wasn't the first nor the last coach to have foibles. Under his guidance we achieved our highest FIFA ranking (4), reached the quarter-finals of the World Cup and the Olympic Games, won the Tournament of Nations and were twice unlucky runners-up in the Asian Cup.

While he was in charge we won fifty-six per cent of our matches and, above all, we were a tightly knit team with an unshakable belief in ourselves and each other. Perhaps that last aspect was the main factor in the decision that he had to go.

I had never met the new, interim coach, Ante Milicic, so I didn't know what to expect or even if he would recall me to the squad.

Ante and I didn't get off on the right foot, and our first meeting really rocked me. He told me that he had doubts about whether there was a role for me in the team. I could understand that he had doubts—after all, I'd had physical and mental challenges that were spoken about openly—but I had now turned a corner and wanted to come back. Despite this, I was being dumped from a Tier 1 to a Tier 3 player, which, apart from being a lot less money, meant I was being demoted to the rank of a young player who had just come into the squad.

Despite his reservations, I was selected in the squad to travel to America for a one-off match against the USA. I knew it was still a long way back into the team, and that I would have to prove my worth off the bench, but at least I had been welcomed back into the fold, as my excited Instagram made clear:

> March 28, 2019: As I sit on the plane to my first National team camp of 2019 with the same butterflies and nerves I felt when I got called in to my first camp, I've sat and reflected on the last few months. For the people that know me well will know that the past 2 years have been the hardest of my life. I found myself in a pretty dark place & the things that made me happy, no longer did. I thought my injury was going to be the tipping point but instead it has become a small blessing. This injury has given me the chance to find myself, my happiness & my love for the game again. I have dealt with my demons, I've grown as a person (not in height 🙄), I have fallen in love with the beautiful game again & I'm ready to see what the next few months have in store for me 💪 We have the best job in the world but I have learnt that we aren't invincible, we are human & we have our struggles just like everyone else. So ask the people around you if they are okay because IT'S OKAY, NOT TO BE OKAY

'Pulsating' and a 'wild ride' are two terms usually used to describe a theme park ride rather than a football match, but that's how journalists saw our match against the USA in Denver, Colorado, in front of 17,000 fans on 4 April 2019.

There is something about our clashes, probably the close physical match-up and style of play combined with our determination to beat the best and their determination to stop us. This match was the epitome of that seesaw battle.

They took the lead through veteran Alex Morgan, who battled her way past defenders to score her one hundredth international goal, but we were learning to be resilient against the world's dominant team and equalised soon after through Lisa De Vanna.

It was still 1–1 at half-time but Caitlin Foord gave us a surprise lead two minutes into the second half, followed soon after by the American reply. It was 2–2 and the match was alight, both sides intent on attack as Megan Rapinoe put the USA ahead on the hour mark, then substitute Mallory Pugh made it 4–2 and we seemed to be losing touch.

Then with nine minutes left Sam Kerr leaped high to meet a cross from Hayley Raso and reduced the deficit to 4–3. An equaliser seemed on the cards as we mounted several attacks before Pugh scored late, on a break from a goal kick against the run of play. I had played little part in the game, coming on in the eighty-ninth minute, but at least I felt part of the team again. *Grateful* was the word I used on social media.

Ante's mood had softened when we talked again after the match. He had faith in me, he insisted, but it was up to me to do the extra training needed to get back up to speed if I was going to be on the team to go to France for the World Cup.

It was the incentive I needed. I went back to Brisbane and began training with the Roar boys. If there was one thing I wasn't afraid of it was hard work and training with men was simply going back to my roots—back to the family backyard and competing against Joel and Daniel.

In mid-May I got the call—I had made it onto the team. I posted on Instagram:

> Six months ago I was physically, mentally and emotionally broken but when a little girl has a dream, nothing can stop that fire from burning. Incredibly grateful to get the opportunity to represent Australia at another World Cup 🏟

As expected, I started on the bench in our first group game against Italy, played in the city of Valenciennes, not far from the Belgian border. It was a match we expected to win, and win well, against a side that was ranked sixteenth and had not qualified to play a World Cup for more than two decades. But, as we would learn, rather than make the Italians pessimistic, those facts would act as a performance spur while we were coming off a worrying 0–3 loss to the Netherlands in a practice match a week earlier.

Still, we began well enough against *Le Azzurre*, playing the attacking brand of football demanded by Ante, which paid dividends when Sam Kerr put us ahead after twenty minutes with a penalty kick that was saved by the Italian keeper before Sam slammed home the rebound. Amazingly, it was Sam's first World Cup goal for the Matildas.

We looked the better side at half-time but the tide turned in the fifty-sixth minute when their star forward Barbara Bonansea pounced on a defensive error and curled home an equaliser which set off a frantic twenty-five minutes of attacks and counter-attacks as both sides sought a win.

I got my chance to play in the sixty-eighth minute, coming on to replace Hayley Raso, as the team tried to hold out an increasingly confident Italy, which had a goal disallowed in the eightieth minute, courtesy of a ruling by the controversial Video Assistant Referee (VAR) system. A draw seemed certain until the last second when Bonansea, who had scored an earlier goal only to have it also denied by VAR, nodded the ball into the net from a free kick to give Italy a win.

Our campaign had got off to a poor start. Ante acknowledged that we needed to regroup and learn from our mistakes. Still, we had dominated possession and made seventeen attempts on goal compared to Italy's five. Things would not be as easy against Brazil, who we now had to beat to stay in the tournament.

We travelled the length of France to play our next match, four days later in the southern city of Montpellier, where more than 17,000 crammed into Stade de la Mosson.

There is a certain, shall we say, *passion* between the two sides and it was on display early with several clashes between players on both sides because we all knew what was at stake. Marta, in particular, was snarling for Brazil and she had the first laugh when she converted a penalty in the twentieth minute after a controversial challenge on midfielder Thaisa Moreno.

Things got worse ten minutes later when forward Cristiane rose above our defenders to nod the ball into the right-hand corner. Things looked bleak; we hadn't played badly but were suddenly 2–0 behind and the tournament was slipping away.

The game settled as we tried to find our way through a tight Brazilian defence now intent on preserving their lead. Then, right on the half-time whistle, Caitlin Foord pounced on a loose ball in the box to score and bring it back to 2–1.

We were suddenly in with a fighting chance. Ante, as calm as usual, told us during the break that we were still in the match and that the second half would determine our World Cup.

The chances kept coming in the second half, both teams realising the importance of the contest. Brazil could seal their place in the knockout stage and we could be going home early if we didn't find the net at least once.

As the hour-mark approached we got the breakthrough when Chloe Logarzo, running down the right flank, crossed the ball looking for Sam Kerr in the middle. Sam couldn't quite reach the ball, but it flashed past her and the Brazilian goalkeeper Barbara and into the net.

With half an hour still to go both sides sought a win as the ball went from end to end. Then Ellie Carpenter tried the same cross as Chloe, looking for Sam in the middle. Fortune was on our side because Sam was in an offside position but didn't touch the ball as it came off the head of Brazilian defender Monica and past a sprawling Barbara to make it 3–2.

We were in front and refused to yield as we held off the South Americans to record probably our best comeback victory. To put our performance in perspective, it was the first time in twenty-four years that a team at the World Cup had come from 2–0 down to win.

'The Matildas are still waltzing', the newspapers cried the next day, praising the comeback. The team was back but I was still on the outer, getting no game time at all against Brazil. One journalist, Ante Jukic from the American television network ESPN, noticed my absence from the pitch and wrote a report that made me blush but also gave me some hope that my skills might again be recognised.

'Katrina Gorry gives the Matildas oxygen,' he wrote.

> Gorry is a unicorn in Australian football. When she was 'herself' [a reference to my admission that I'd had a difficult few years], her combination of positional sense, technique and decision-making in midfield was entirely unique in Australian football. It's little wonder that the Matildas' middling form the past year correlated with her gradual move to the periphery under Alen Stajcic. There has never been a player, male or female, like her in the Australian game—never that refined in that position. Deeper in central midfield, Gorry has the

> ability to attract defenders and create separation from them in tight space, leading to better openings for the collective. Her play is defined by short and explosive dribbles, assertive movement and an ability to progress the ball as well as keep it. That's everything a penetrative and effective midfielder needs in football today to create domino effects during phases of possession in the defensive and middle thirds.

I doubt that Ante Milicic read the article but I was back in the starting team for our last group match against Jamaica in the city of Grenoble, a three-hour bus ride from Montpellier. The match would become known for Sam Kerr's four goals, and I was very pleased to provide the assist for her second which gave me a sense of relief that I could still play an important role in the team's midfield.

Jamaica came back in the second half and scored a goal of their own—their first in World Cup finals—before Sam restored our two-goal buffer by claiming her hat-trick in a goalmouth scramble.

The other group match between Brazil and Italy was being played in Valenciennes at the same time and there were some nervous moments when Brazil scored to lead 1–0, which meant they had a better goal difference than us, but Sam came to the rescue with seven minutes left when she pounced on a mistake by the Jamaican goalkeeper to score her fourth and ensure that we finished above Brazil on goal difference.

The result meant we would play Norway, ranked twelfth and who finished second in their group, in the round of sixteen instead of England, who were ranked third and had won all three of their group matches. The match was in the city of Nice but I would play no part in it as Ante left me sitting on the bench, my recall a fleeting one.

Sam almost scored off the starting manoeuvre, her shot after twenty-five seconds just missing the left-hand netting as we dominated possession for most of the first half. As happens sometimes with dominance, we came to regret a series of near-misses as Norway took their one clear chance when forward Isabell Herlovsen squeezed in between two defenders and thumped it past Lydia Williams.

We continued to press in the second half as Hayley, Caitlin and Sam missed chances. It felt like we were going to fall short before Elise Kellond-Knight curled a corner kick in low to the near post where it bounced and evaded everyone before rolling into the goal.

We were back on level terms and full-time a few minutes later meant half an hour of extra time. Alanna Kennedy was red-carded soon after and we were left with only ten players to hold out the increasingly confident Norwegians who began to have misses themselves.

We managed to hold on and hoped we could win the penalty lottery that would follow.

Norway won the toss, went first through Caroline Graham Hansen and scored. Sam stepped up to lead the

Matildas' response and missed, not *just* missed but missed by miles as she skied the ball into the crowd. Norway's Guro Reiten made it 2–0 which put even more pressure on Emily Gielnik, whose shot was saved by the keeper. I understood how she felt as the Norwegian captain, Maren Mjelde, made it 3–0. Steph Catley made no mistake but it now depended on whether Lydia could save Norway's last two penalties. She couldn't as Ingrid Engen converted to end our dream. Our preparation may have been affected by Alen Stajcic's sacking but we had still come to France believing we had the talent to win the tournament and instead we had not even reached the quarter-finals.

The loss was as bad as our penalty loss to Brazil at the Olympics three years earlier. Perhaps even worse.

We headed home unsure of the future. Ante's appointment had been a temporary measure so it was possible that we might have yet another new coach within a few months.

On a personal note, my return to the squad had been patchy. I felt that I hadn't been given the time on the pitch to make my mark. I was again left out in two friendlies in November against Chile and I finished the year searching for a way to convince Ante that I deserved another chance.

The one promising note was that the first match at Parramatta on 9 November attracted a record-breaking crowd of over 20,000. The team might have underperformed in France but the public support was growing, and growing quickly. I desperately wanted to be a part of it.

CHAPTER NINETEEN

My Roomie

There is a long-standing tradition that elite athletes on tour in a team generally room with another player. It is not only a cost-saving measure—which was particularly important for the Matildas when I was first selected—but it can also help build team camaraderie and ensure that young people always have someone with them.

When Hesterine de Reus took the Matildas to Europe in 2014 to play the Netherlands and France, she announced at the camp that we were all going to change our room partners, and she was going to choose who roomed with who. The announcement was part of her desire to call the shots and shake up the team after the Tom Sermanni era to create a 'professional' environment.

As you can imagine, the order was greeted with some protest by many players. A 'roomie'—your hotel room partner during training camps and tours—is one of the most important relationships within a sporting team, and to mess with a settled group of friendships was bound to cause a level of disharmony.

The roomie relationship is a bit like a marriage. Normal friendships can exist quite happily on the basis that you see someone occasionally, usually in a social environment where you share a certain level of private information. But a roomie is someone you spend most of your time with—awake or asleep—where 'personal' has a far more intimate connotation.

I was still relatively new to the team and had had different roomies on tours, but Hesterine decided that the person who would share with me was Michelle Heyman. I have no idea why—perhaps it was because there was a natural relationship on the field between me playing in the number 10 role and Michelle playing number 9—but it was a decision that created a friendship, a bond, that changed both our lives.

You just have to look at Michelle and she makes you happy. She has an impossibly wide smile that starts and finishes with her eyes. And behind that happy, optimistic exterior is a kind and caring person who has your back on and off the field. I made an emotional video when she told me in 2019 that she was retiring and I cried again, this time with joy, five years later when she came back into the national team.

I asked Michelle to talk about our friendship as part of this book, the good times and the difficult.

'I'd known Mini since the early days of the W-League when she played for Adelaide and I played for Canberra. Things were quite relaxed back then and we often went out with opposing teams after a match. I always thought that Mini was fun to be around, always smiling and having a good time. She had energy and people wanted to be around her, so when we became room-mates it was as if we had known each other forever without actually knowing each other deeply.

'That's the thing—I don't think a lot of people understand how difficult it is to find someone that you can live with for weeks and even months at a time without getting on each other's nerves. It's not as if there is an entire house in which to find your own space; most hotel rooms are roughly twenty square metres.

'Our friendship blossomed from day one and I think the reason we have got on so well is that we are very similar. Outside, with the team, she is this funny, energetic little bunny, but once we get into the room she becomes quiet and laid-back, with a chill out vibe. We can find contentment in each other's company whether we are watching a movie or just lying on the bed talking. It's a time to recharge, and we rarely even talk about football.

'I am so grateful for every minute we've spent in those rooms, even Hesterine's mandatory, enforced afternoon nap times. We've had lots of wonderful, happy times together but there have also been some terrible times where we've been important to each other. It was important having your person there, especially when we were away from home for so long. We felt safe with each other and could talk about whatever we needed to feel good, and to be able to perform as athletes.

'We both have had our struggles, and I think there was a point where we were both going through a pretty bad time together. In 2018, I was physically drained, battling a number of injuries and mentally fed up with the system and what was going on at that time. Mini and I could talk to each other freely in that situation, if only in that we felt safe to get everything off our chests.

'I remember being in Jordan in April that year for the Asian Cup, standing at the hotel window staring out at the city and lamenting: "I am a thirty-year-old woman, what am I doing? The coach hates me, I can't get a game—it's time to retire."

'Mini and I sat and discussed my options and she convinced me to stay and see things through. It was not the time to be making such big decisions when I was feeling so low, she insisted. Mini was my person whom I trust like no other, and she was right.

'I know she feels the same way about me because we used to discuss Joel and his drug problems a lot. It weighed heavily on her because she felt as if she should be there, alongside him. Even during his worst period, Joel would call Mini before every game and wish her well and tell her how proud he was of her. I think that shows how close the Gorry family are to each other.

'There was one conversation I remember in particular, when Joel was in rehab and his room-mate hanged himself. It scared the shit out of Mini—the realisation that a person could take their own life, and that it could have been Joel. She was helpless on the other side of the world, trapped because of a commitment to football. Thankfully, what was a horrible situation ended up helping Joel turn his life around.

'It was much more difficult to reach Mini over her eating disorder. There were mornings when she would get out of bed at 5 am, put on a rain jacket and go out for a long run *before* training. I would hear the clunk of the hotel room door as she left and know that she'd gone out to sweat and to try to make herself feel good.

'Then at meal times I would watch her fill her plate with food and then sit and pretend to eat; first move the food around the plate and then put a little bit in her mouth and move it around as if she was chewing but she'd never actually eat anything. She was eating but she wasn't actually eating.

'I didn't want to put any extra pressure on her, to force a conversation, but I could see that she was in real pain about herself. After we returned to Australia I called the team psych one night because I was so worried. I knew it wasn't normal and she desperately needed help. Even if she wasn't coming directly to me for help, I knew that it was time to step in. I couldn't bear seeing her so sad about herself, and I didn't want her to fade away. The next day Mini messaged me to say thank you so I knew I had done the right thing.

'It's part of the life of an elite athlete. No matter what is happening in your private life—and we all go through the same pressures as other people—you have to switch on at game time to perform. It's like turning on a light, and you have to be able to manage those feelings.

'I could see sometimes that Mini's pressures off the field would show in the ferocity of her tackles, as if in her anger she used her worries and frustrations in a positive way to fuel her performance and tenacity.

'Mini is good at hiding feelings although sometimes they have shown themselves in a bad way. The worst was after we lost to Brazil at the Olympics in 2016 and Mini had a penalty saved. It was clear that she really felt responsible for the Matildas not being in the semi-finals and she went out drinking with some of the team afterwards.

'I went out for a short while but then went back to the hotel. I didn't want to celebrate losing or drink my sorrows, it's just not me, but Mini stayed out and got really drunk. She eventually had to be carried back to the hotel. She was in a bad way and I remember being very angry about it.

'The next morning I called one of our team managers and told him: "You're booking two tickets home today for me and Mini", which he did. I then told Mini that we were going home and missing the closing ceremony. "I don't trust you," I said, honestly scared for her life. I needed to protect her from herself.

'Motherhood has changed everything, of course. Mini was talking about being a mum from the early days, even that she would retire at twenty-three if she had to because she wanted it so much. I told her that there was no way I'd let her retire so early, and I'm so glad things worked out the way they have.

'As far as on-field is concerned, she is a player who would never, ever give up. I think her heart is bigger than anything else in her body. If she misses a tackle then she runs back to make sure that she gets the next one. If she makes a bad pass then she doesn't hang her shoulders but makes sure that the next pass is a good one. She helps out and never seems to tire.

'Our relationship on the field is similar to our relationship as room-mates in that we don't have to talk to communicate. For a lot of the time we've played as number 9 and number 10 positions, so our link-up play is very important. Ever since I've come back onto the team, initially for the 2024 Olympic Games, our coach Tony Gustavsson has noticed at training how much we understand each other.

'I just have to look at her and she knows instinctively what sort of run I'm going to make. If I looked back at the goals I've scored for the Matildas then it wouldn't surprise me if most of them didn't involve Mini in some way.

'She's creative and smart in the midfield where she can control the play and create chances. She would make a great captain.'

CHAPTER TWENTY

'What? You're Pregnant?'

Clare Polkinghorne and I had both signed with Norwegian club Avaldsnes in January 2020, keen to have our first experience of European football with an eye on the Tokyo Olympics, scheduled for the middle of the year.

Avaldsnes had finished runners-up in Norway's top-flight league, the Toppserien, between 2015 and 2017 but since then had fallen back into the middle of the pack. Our signings were part of a push by the club to get back to the top of the league and qualify for the UEFA Champions League.

Like the Ottawa Fury in Canada, where I had played eight years before, Avaldsnes had a history of signing Australians. Clare and I had a hard act to follow because Tameka Yallop (née Butt) had spent the previous three seasons there, during which she scored an incredible thirty-two goals.

But then Covid struck and the season, along with everything else, was delayed due to lockdowns. Clare and I twiddled our fingers back in Australia until we were finally given a special clearance to travel.

Nothing could really prepare me for my arrival. Avaldsnes is actually a small town on the island of Karmoy, the westernmost part of Norway, known for its heather moors and white sand surf beaches (a little colder than Queensland!). It's connected to the mainland by a tunnel and a bridge. The town has barely 2000 residents but is full of Viking history, and it would be my home for the next six months. Unfortunately, when the season finally got underway in July, the matches were mostly played in empty venues due to Covid.

The team began well enough with a solid win and I found myself selected in the league's team of the week. It was a positive beginning and we would stay in the hunt for the title for most of the season. I played in thirteen of the eighteen games and scored three goals but I was injured towards the end of the season and had to sit and watch as we faded to finish third, frustratingly close to a Champions League berth.

My injury had come from nowhere during a game, the pain lancing through me like a knife. It was diagnosed as osteitis pubis, an inflammation of the pubic area probably caused by my active lifestyle, and I had no choice but to rest it to allow the inflammation to subside. I went from being part of a team involved in an exciting end of the season to doing rehab alone in an empty gym.

It was in this moment, far from home and still in a quandary about football, that my thoughts wandered. Instead of going to bed each night and dreaming about the match ahead, my dreams were filled with potential baby names.

I was in a relationship at the time and had made it clear when we got together how strongly I felt about having a family. At first she had gone along with the idea but now, two years on, she had changed her mind and called me one night to say that she couldn't make the commitment to have kids.

That was it for me and the relationship ended then and there. I was sad but, in a strange way, a weight had been lifted and I could now make a decision without having to consider anyone else.

I was working with a life coach, trying to work out what was missing from my life, and all I could come up with was a baby. 'Well, maybe this is your path,' he said. 'Why don't you just do it.' It was a statement rather than a question.

I had long felt that 2021 was going to be the right time for me to have a baby. It would be the year after the Tokyo Olympics, which would allow me time to be pregnant and give birth, and, all being well, to get back to the game in time for the 2023 World Cup and the 2024 Paris Olympics.

Covid had changed that scenario, pushing back the Tokyo Games to July 2021. I had been a member of the team that qualified for the Games so I had a decision to make—Olympics or baby.

The answer was clear and a few days later I made an appointment at a private IVF fertility clinic in the nearby town of Haugesund. I didn't tell anyone about my plan, not family, friends or team-mates. This was something I was doing on my own and I didn't want anyone trying to talk me out of it.

The strangest thing happened on the morning of the appointment. I had been tracking my periods very closely and wasn't due for another two weeks but as I walked through the clinic door, I got my period. It was so unlike me. When I sat down, I told the male doctor. He looked at me and said, 'That means we can start today.'

I looked at him, wide-eyed. Even though I desperately wanted to have a baby, I thought this was just an introductory meeting and the process would take some time. I hadn't really prepared myself to make a decision at that moment but there was nowhere to go now and there would be no going back. I realised that this was meant to be.

'Why not,' I replied.

The only question now was about the donor. What did I want, the doctor asked. Some people like to know what the donor looks like—if they are tall, fit or good at something. Some couples even like to choose a donor who may resemble their partner. But my reply was simple. Beyond being a Scandinavian (I love the Scandi look), I just wanted the donor to be healthy. The rest didn't matter to me. At the end of the day, it's how you parent your child that matters, so a mysterious and anonymous donor was perfect, although I did make sure he was an open donor so that, after she has turned eighteen, Harper can decide if she wants to meet her genetic father.

The process began with a series of injections of the hormone FSH over ten days or so to stimulate my ovaries to produce more and better eggs in preparation for the transfer of the embryo. I was so excited that I videoed myself doing the first injection.

'Day one of this journey,' I told my iPhone camera before taking a deep breath, pinching my stomach and inserting the needle. Looking back, it gives me goosebumps because I can see the joy on my face. I had been telling people about this moment for more than half my life and now it was here.

I was living with three team-mates and I wanted to keep the IVF a secret, so I had to hide my injections in an ice-cream container at the back of the fridge and hope that no one else opened it. I also had to find excuses to sneak out to attend my appointments.

I had already booked my post-season flight back to Australia, which couldn't be changed because flights were limited during Covid. At the clinic, everything was timed so I would receive the embryo the day before leaving, but the FSH response was slow so the doctors wanted another day before giving the final trigger shot to ensure my body was ready. That, in turn, put back the embryo transfer by a day—the day I was leaving Norway.

Things were getting a little tricky.

The nurses agreed to open the clinic early so I had time to receive the transfer before racing to the airport. I had to make up a story to tell my flatmates that I was going out to collect the results of blood tests I'd done because of Covid travel restrictions. One of my flatmates wanted to drive me and I had to insist that I would do it myself, which weirded her out.

To make matters worse, it had begun to snow, which made me anxious about flight cancellations. Thankfully, the embryo transfer only took a few minutes so I made my flight and flopped into my seat, relieved but with my head still in a whirlwind.

Normally I would curl up and go to sleep on a plane, but this time it would be a sleepless trip for me all the way back to Brisbane. I sat with my legs crossed because I had got it into my head that the embryo might fall out. It's funny in hindsight, but that's how much I cared.

My return to Queensland was no secret, the Brisbane Roar having already announced publicly that I would play the season back in the team's orange strip. Coach Jake Goodship was very welcoming.

'Katrina has been one of the league's finest footballers for some time now and she has been an incredible player for Brisbane Roar over many years,' he told the club's fan site. 'It's an exciting signing for the club. To have a player of Katrina's calibre back in Australia, back in Brisbane, well done to everyone involved in making it happen. The fans will love it.'

My choice of words in the article was interesting considering my personal situation: 'I am a family person. I have a lot of them, and some newborns in the family too [my sister Amanda had recently had a baby], so I needed to come home and stay home.'

I had made the comments and finalised the contract before my decision to undergo the IVF treatment. As my flight descended into Brisbane Airport, I wondered about the best course of action. Should I come clean or stay mum, if you'll excuse the pun.

I decided on the latter—to wait and see. If the embryo didn't take, as I expected from my reading about IVF, then I would play the season with Roar and perhaps try again later in the year when I returned to Norway. If I became pregnant then I would keep playing while it was safe to do so and Jake believed I was valuable to the team.

Australia was still in the grip of lockdowns and hotel quarantines so there was no one to welcome me at the airport. No hugs and shrieks and kisses from family and friends. The arrival hall was empty as myself and the other passengers were processed and marched by security guards to waiting buses and then transported to city hotels where we were quarantined for two weeks.

I was staying at the Meriton, four walls and food delivery left in brown paper bags in the corridor, while Queenslanders were going about their daily business outside in the glorious sunshine that I missed so much.

I settled in and phoned Mum to say I'd arrived and was feeling good. There was no point saying anything else at this stage. Can you imagine if I had told her: 'Oh, by the way I've just had an embryo inserted and I'm hoping to get pregnant.'

Over the next few days I began to feel really sick. At first I put it down to a bug but the nausea became worse and worse.

Anxiety got the better of me and I began doing pregnancy tests each morning, even though I knew it was too early to be able to tell accurately. On the fourth morning I took the test and then left the strip sitting on the kitchen bench while I went into the bedroom. I came back twenty minutes later to find that a faint second line had appeared.

I squealed with delight, but then my doubts set in. The line was very faint and I had left the test too long, which meant it could give a false reading as the urine dried away. I couldn't hold back any longer and excitedly phoned my sister, Amanda, and told her everything, from the secret IVF to the faint line on the pregnancy test.

'What does it mean?' I asked anxiously. 'Did I leave it too long?'

'You might have,' she replied. 'Be patient and check it again in a couple of days.'

There was no doubt when I tested again. The line was now dark from the traces of the hCG hormone. I was definitely pregnant. I remember sitting on the bed and bursting into tears. Joyful tears. I couldn't believe that this was actually happening.

It was time to make it real, so I sent a text message to my best friend, Jade, saying that I had a present for her. 'You didn't have to do that,' she texted back, thinking I'd brought her a Christmas gift from Norway. We then FaceTimed.

When I came onscreen with Jade, I was holding the positive pregnancy test up to the camera so she could see the line. At first she was confused—what? how? who?—but when I explained what had happened, I swear there were tears in her eyes. She was so happy as she told me how proud she was.

'It's typical of you,' she said. 'You've been telling me for years that you would go ahead no matter what, and with or without a partner, and you have.' Those words meant a lot to me.

It was time to tell my other siblings—Daniel, Joel and my younger brother Lachlan, whose wife, Remy, already suspected something was afoot because I'd asked her to drop off some things for me at the hotel when I'd arrived, including some pregnancy test kits. She'd never asked why but must have had an inkling. They were all excited for me. After all, I'd been talking about it since we were children.

Mum was a different matter. Amanda and I decided it was best to tell her when I came out of quarantine rather than on the phone. It was a big deal after all. Amanda would film her response, which turned out to be hilarious.

Mum was puzzled when I put a box on the kitchen bench at home and asked her to open it. Inside there were baby booties and the results of the pregnancy tests.

'Whose is this?' she asked, frowning.

I smiled back. 'Mine.'

'What? You're pregnant?'

'Yep.'

'When did you fall pregnant? How?'

Amanda was trying to hold her iPhone camera steady as she started giggling at Mum's surprise. My mum simply had no idea that I would do something like this. I guess she never thought I was serious about it—until now. We were all crying and laughing and hugging, but her questions continued.

'How far pregnant are you?'

'Four weeks.'

'But what about your football?'

'Mum, this is the best decision I've ever made in my life.'

Dad's response was hilarious too. I dropped over the next day for breakfast and walked in carrying a shoebox. Inside was a positive pregnancy test, baby socks with *Grandma and Grandad* written on them and a baby jumpsuit with the word *Mini* on it. Michelle understood immediately, but Dad was confused and thought I was opening a cafe called Mini's. When he got over the shock, he was immediately supportive because he knew what it meant to me.

—

I had spent the final week in quarantine thinking about the practicalities of my decision. Even though football had been my obsession since I was six years old, it was the thought of motherhood that made me happy.

I needed this change in my life, and if it meant being finished with football then so be it. It was meant to be. I had achieved a lot in the game already: playing in premiership teams, for overseas clubs and for my country, so if it ended here then I was cool with that.

My behaviour had already changed as I developed an almost immediate craving for hot chips. I ate them for breakfast, lunch and dinner for the next three months, which sounds ridiculous for an elite athlete and someone who had endured bulimia. But I was happy to give in and enjoy the moment.

I didn't immediately break the news to my team-mates and the coaching staff, but by the third game of the season I could sense that I was close to calling it quits. I hadn't wanted to say anything until the twelve-week mark of my pregnancy but by now I was exhausted, both my body and mind starting to feel the strain. The girls and my coach Jake reacted amazingly, happy and excited for me and encouraging me to come back to the game when I was ready.

I played the next match against Canberra and, as it happened, the ball fell to me about thirty metres out from goal. It was only three minutes into the match and I decided to shoot, striking it perfectly high into the top right-hand corner.

'It's a trademark, long-range goal from Katrina Gorry,' the television commentator called as I was mobbed by my team-mates. Even our goalkeeper Georgina Worth ran the length of the field to join in.

It looked like an over-the-top goal celebration, but my team-mates' enthusiasm was all about my baby news. It was one of the most cherished moments in my life because I knew that they had my back. I played one more time before stepping away from the game to concentrate on the birth.

The Matildas were also supportive, accepting my decision and encouraging me to come back to the team when I was ready, but at this point I was truly uncertain about what would happen next.

I approached pregnancy the same way I had approached football, with as much attention to detail as possible. As far as I was concerned, if I did the right things and informed myself properly, then I could handle anything. I found out that I was having a daughter. She now had an identity. She was Harper.

Over the next six months I did as much research as I could. I listened to a lot of podcasts. I did hypno-birthing classes and I spoke at length to Mum and Amanda about their experiences.

I had it all planned, or so I thought. I don't think I realised how quickly your body can change. Cravings are weird. I was a vegan and all I craved was meat. Now I eat meat. I craved salty, carby food like hot chips. I tried to make myself salads and I'd look at them and want to be sick. It was a really strange feeling.

As an athlete, you often feel invincible, so seeing my body change so quickly was difficult to experience. But my dismay was countered by my fascination with pregnancy, how incredibly cool it is that the human body can build and then feed a baby and keep it alive.

I wanted to keep everything about the pregnancy and birth as natural as possible, to feel every moment of this amazing experience of giving life. I wasn't interested in taking drugs to dull the pain of childbirth. It was supposed to hurt, wasn't it, so why would I shy away from something that was an integral part of the experience? I could handle pain, I told myself.

My waters broke on my twenty-ninth birthday, the 13th of August. I was watching the Tokyo Olympics on TV and I actually thought I had weed my pants. I was like, 'Oh, that's awkward . . . wait, does that mean I'm in labour?'

I was so excited, particularly when I started having contractions, but then nothing more happened. My back was really sore so I decided to distract myself by painting my belly and dancing in the hope that the movement would spark some activity from within. But still nothing. Harper wasn't budging from her warm surroundings and I would just have to wait a little longer.

The next day I went to the Mater Mothers' Hospital in Brisbane and the doctors decided that I should be induced because I wasn't dilating enough to have the baby naturally. I didn't want that to happen because it changes the nature of your labour.

To make matters worse, the baby, who had been in a good position for my whole pregnancy, decided to turn and was 'OP', or what they call sunny side up, which means the baby's head is down but facing my abdomen. This means that, because of the angle, its head is larger for the delivery.

Just what I needed—not.

Suddenly, the pain in my back was like nothing I'd experienced before. They gave me a morphine shot, but it didn't do much. Then came the water shots, which is four needles in your back to take the pain away. They were excruciating at first, but they gave me some relief.

Two hours later, the drugs had worn off and the pain returned. I asked for another morphine shot. It had been twelve hours, and I was still in pain, even after they gave me an epidural. All my expectations for labour were now out of the window—I'd gone from not wanting any drugs to having the lot.

Another three hours passed before I realised that Harper was finally ready to come out. The doctors started to get worried, because my temperature was spiking and the baby was still in there, falling asleep during the contractions.

I was lucky to have such a good obstetrician who knew I didn't want a C-section. I remember her looking at me and saying, 'I believe in you, we're going to push this baby out.'

Eventually, after another three hours of pushing, I was able to deliver Harper myself. I reached down, pulled her up and held her close.

Harper Ollie Gorry came into the world six days overdue but healthy. Meanwhile, I was a total mess. My eyes were heavy and I had lost a litre of blood. I was even vomiting up blood. I was so tired that I started thinking about asking someone to hold Harper for me. I still feel guilty about this. But then I looked down and saw her face and decided I couldn't let her go. I think that's what pulled me through.

When I was in the clear, I looked over to my mum, who'd had five kids without drugs. 'I don't know how you did it. You're my hero,' I said.

CHAPTER TWENTY-ONE

Breastfeeding in Boots

I have always liked the name Frankie. It's gender-neutral and has attitude—perfect, particularly if I had a daughter.

That was my plan, but at some point in my pregnancy, maybe around the twelve-week mark, I came across the name Harper. Maybe it was the link with Harper Lee, author of the great American novel *To Kill a Mockingbird*, but somehow it stuck with me, and when I realised that a lot of my friends had dogs called Frankie or Franklin, I decided to switch.

Harper's middle name—Ollie—is much more personal. My late maternal grandmother's name was Olive, although she was known to everyone as Ollie. Grandma was a big part of my life and very supportive of my football. I thought about her a lot, and the two names seemed to go naturally together.

So Harper Ollie Gorry it would be, and when she finally arrived, I knew her name was just right. As traumatic as they were, those three days from the moment my waters broke to my first cuddle with Harper were some of the most incredible moments of my life.

Childbirth changes you mentally and physically. I had been through the darkness of depression, an eating disorder and body image issues but this was something completely different. The way I bounced back after pregnancy gave me a new appreciation for what the female body can do. It was exhilarating.

I probably should have already realised this while I was playing football, because as athletes we push ourselves to the limit, but it took being pregnant and having a baby for me to feel proud of my body. This was especially true for breastfeeding and the feeling of knowing that I'm responsible for keeping us both healthy and alive. The body is not just something to look at, or to be looked at, it has a purpose. And it's a purpose that is to be cherished, something that is too often ignored by a society captured by shallow advertising and expectations.

Going through pregnancy, labour, childbirth and post-pregnancy made me feel unstoppable. All my negative emotions and questions about myself disappeared and I now knew that my life contained two joys—Harper and football.

As I'd discovered with my earlier injury, having time away from the game was refreshing. Life as a new mother was exactly as I had pictured it. My sleeping was long and restful, with Harper beside me, and fretful mornings to get to training were replaced by happy walks along the Brisbane River with our puppy Rio. Time was to be enjoyed rather than managed and the fact that I had done this alone, as I had promised myself for so many years, just made it sweeter.

It also made me realise that I missed football, and that as much as I wanted to be a mum, I was also a sportsperson who needed to play the game I loved. Before Harper, I had been in a professional environment, doing the same things over and over again, which can be tedious. Football was no longer my entire life but rather a part of it, and somehow that made me appreciate it more. I now wanted to be able to combine these two very different needs in my life to make me a whole person.

The first challenge was to return to match fitness, a task I understood and relished. I was doing Pilates within a few weeks of Harper's birth and was back running two months later, slowly building momentum with the help of a physio. Even the osteitis pubis had disappeared, as if my body had been reset.

As soon as I started running I remembered the feeling I used to have that I could go on forever. I felt so different, and like I could do anything I wanted. It was such a relief to finally trust my body again, and to feel it grow stronger day by day. It was the fittest and healthiest I have ever felt, and I had developed much more appreciation for my body's capabilities and needs.

Three months later I was back training with my Brisbane Roar team-mates to be ready for the A-League campaign, which kicked off in early December 2021. Now for the hard part—being a breastfeeding mum wearing football boots.

Luckily, Mum came to the rescue again. She had graduated from mother bus driver who shared parental duties taking her kids to their matches each weekend to grandmother babysitter, the figure in the distance wheeling Harper around the football field in her pram during training sessions and waiting outside the change rooms during matches in case I was needed to give Harper a top-up.

Whatever my misgivings about the way my parents responded to me coming out as gay, their love and support for my life choices, good and not so good, could never be questioned.

Probably the most wonderful aspect of my return to the Brisbane team was the encouragement I received from my team-mates and coaches, particularly as I was treading in unknown territory to some extent.

There had been football mums before me, although none had made the decision that I had taken to go solo. Their experiences were mixed. Some were positive, like Amy Rodriguez, my former team-mate in Kansas who'd had two children, the first in 2013 and then another in 2016, and was welcomed back into the US national team on both occasions. Others had a more difficult time, like Iceland captain Sara Björk Gunnarsdóttir, who took her French club Lyon to court, and won, over being underpaid while on maternity leave. Former Matildas goalkeeper Melissa Barbieri claimed that she lost her funding and contracts after having a daughter in 2013 and Katie Chapman, former England player and mother of two boys, was dropped and had her central contract cancelled in 2010 when she took a brief break to be with her family.

By contrast, Brisbane welcomed me back, with praise. Head coach Garrath McPherson even described me as a role model and mentioned Harper by name.

'It is wonderful to have Katrina back in orange for the upcoming season,' he told the media when my return was announced. 'We are excited to have her and Harper join the team. She will be a leader for our younger players and is a role model for the next generation coming through Brisbane Roar and the Matildas. We are excited to support her as she returns to professional football after starting her family and look forward to creating an environment that enables her to thrive.'

I was ecstatic. 'The Roar is home for me. I love being part of the team with the supporters we have and I love calling Brisbane home. I'm excited to come back for my tenth season. It's a different bunch of girls, which is always exciting. New people bring new personalities and new flair to the team.'

We decided to play safe and schedule my first game back with the team perhaps in the third match of the season, particularly as the first match was over in Perth against the Glory and I had never flown with Harper.

But plans are often overridden by reality. I was at my aunt's house the day before the game and received a phone call from the club. One of my team-mates had been stopped at Perth Airport because of a Covid test and had to return home. We were a player short to fill out the team sheet and I was needed so we wouldn't have to forfeit.

As usual, Mum dropped everything to come with us as we caught an early flight the next day, unsure how things would go with Harper who was now four months old. It was amazing; she was so chill the whole way and her dummy worked a treat to help with her ears as the plane descended into Perth.

Even so, I hadn't had much sleep from worrying about the trip and felt a bit spaced out, as if I'd overdosed on caffeine. There wasn't much time between arriving and the kick-off so I was still out of it when we got into the change rooms to prepare for the game. At one point I went to kick one of the little trigger balls they use for massage, completely missed and fell over. Everyone was like, 'Are you okay?'

I wasn't really and sat on the bench hoping I wouldn't be called into the game but knowing that I probably would be, if only to give me a little game time. I came on as a substitute midway through the second half as we protected a 1–0 lead in front of a decent crowd of about 1000.

I was still struggling and couldn't really get into the game although I had a few touches and enjoyed the sense that I was back with the team. Sadly, there was no fairytale ending as Glory scored twice in the dying minutes, including an own goal right on full-time. It is a long flight home when you lose, but at least I was back playing.

Glory followed us across the Nullarbor for the reverse fixture a week later in front of a crowd of well over 2000 who gave me a big cheer when I came on in the fifty-fifth minute. The match was tight with neither side able to score.

The extra week had made a big difference for me. I'd had time to prepare properly for the game and felt that I had an influence from the moment I came onto the ground. Unlike the previous week when I'd felt overwhelmed, this time I wanted to get involved and get onto the ball as much as possible.

I was playing a much more forward role, happy to run around across the top of the box until an opportunity arose and I let rip with a shot from thirty-five metres out, only to see it tipped around the post by their goalkeeper. I had another shot, which was blocked, as the team started creating chances. Unfortunately, they were all denied and when Glory had their own opportunity with a couple of minutes to play, they scored.

Two last-gasp losses to start the season was hard to take but we were a young squad and took some heart from the performances. I was feeling pretty good about my return and Harper seemed to be coping as well. I knew that I belonged out there on the pitch again and that I could work my way back to the player I was before, if not better.

My first full match was the last game before the Christmas break, against Canberra away from home. For the third time we came unstuck in the final few minutes as a 3–1 lead disappeared and we had to settle for a 3–3 draw, our first points for the season.

We had a change in fortune after the New Year when we beat Melbourne Victory away from home. Finally it was our turn to play well at the end of the game. I scored from the top of the box in the eighty-sixth minute—my first goal since returning—and we scored twice more after that to win 4–2.

Two weeks later I scored the winner against the Wellington Phoenix with a converted penalty, of all things. I hated the idea of taking the kick but it was important to play the role of a senior player and make the most of the opportunity. I didn't wait around for someone to make a decision, instead I grabbed the ball and headed to the spot. I tried to block out the awful memories of Rio and just concentrate on striking it sweetly. I was always going to go left and low because it is my natural sweep of the leg. The whistle sounded, I ran in and slotted it home.

I scored another penalty two weeks later, this time against Melbourne City, and my improving form seemed to be noticed when I was named in the Matildas team to travel to India for the Asian Cup.

It was a surprise really. I had not expected it to happen so soon. But it was also the first time that my two lives clashed and one had to give way to the other. I relinquished my place in the team simply because of the risk to Harper travelling overseas with Covid still rampant and into an environment that was questionable for a five-month-old baby. The decision was easy in the end; there was no doubt in my mind that no matter how much I loved the game, being a mother was my number one priority.

Besides, I knew there would be other opportunities, in particular the World Cup, which was being hosted by Australia and New Zealand in 2023, and by which time, Harper would be almost two years old.

Instead, I concentrated on the Roar where I'd been made vice-captain. It was a wonderful chance for me to have a mentoring role, to think about my team-mates rather than focusing on my own performance and mistakes. I have always been hard on myself, infatuated with what I did wrong rather than the good things, and this was a chance to get out of my own head.

I really tried to help the younger girls in that season to think differently and to be there if they needed me for a bit of confidence and self-belief. It also changed the way I thought of myself as a leader and how I could actually impact the game, not just as a player but off the field as well.

The team finished mid-table for the season, which was a decent effort with such a young squad. I won the Players' Player award, which was very touching. You could see how much it meant to me in the photo Mum took of me after the last game, the trophy in one hand and Harper in my arms. It seemed that my two worlds *could* co-exist.

My international comeback match would be in April 2022 in a friendly against New Zealand held in Townsville in front of a noisy crowd who gave me a great reception as the teams came out onto the ground.

It was an unbelievable feeling. Here I was, a single mum with a baby and somehow back playing for my country. I felt lighter and happier, less worried about immediate results and kinder on myself. I think it also made me more open and able to relax my guard a little.

But the added pressure of an international made me tense and Harper could feel my anxiety as I tried to breastfeed in the sheds before the game. For once she refused to latch on and just looked up at me and smiled as the clock ticked down to game time.

We were in an overflow room so the rest of the team couldn't see what was going on. Mum had come down from the stands and was trying to distract Harper, which wasn't working. In my frustration I yelled at her to get out of the room because 'you're only making it worse'.

It was all getting stressful but thankfully Harper got on the breast and I managed to give her some milk before handing her to Mum and rushing to join the others who were ready to go out onto the ground.

When I finally got into the game that night I felt untouchable, running around with seemingly endless energy in an incredible match. We had thirty-seven shots on goal but were denied by the Kiwis until injury time when we scored two late goals to clinch the match.

As we huddled together after the game, captain Sam Kerr insisted that we deserved the win despite the late goals.

'Let's enjoy it,' she shouted as we all cheered. 'And welcome back Mini, you were amazing.' I was on top of the world as Mum came out onto the ground, crying happily as she carried Harper who was asleep in her arms despite the noise in the stadium.

Our victory against the Ferns was a little easier in Canberra four days later when we scored three goals before half-time. I felt comfortable being back in the team, but although the result was clinical, the two matches highlighted the complexity of my situation with Harper.

Mum and I had never discussed the details of how football was going to look in my life with Harper, but as soon as I got the call-up for the national team, she said simply:

'All right, I'm coming with you.' On the rare occasions that she wasn't available we got a nanny or my stepmother, Michelle, helped out at times.

I breastfed Harper for the first year. Although she was an incredibly easy baby and seemed to adapt to what was going on around her, my breasts were often sore and I would cringe at the thought of getting elbowed in the chest or the ball hitting me. I would often end matches with bruises. Still, that was the price I had to pay, and a bit of pain never worried me too much.

Harper was a ravenous baby and at times it felt as if she was sucking the life out of me. I had put on twenty-five kilos during the pregnancy but within three months of having Harper, I shed it all and dropped back to fifty-one kilos. This was a problem for me as an athlete because, although I felt great out on the field, I needed to regain muscle if I was going to get back to my best. As soon as I stopped breastfeeding I really noticed the difference, particularly with the strength in my legs, which is what I need for speed and power. My jump scores for a vertical leap increased from thirty-two centimetres to thirty-nine centimetres.

It wasn't just my own return to match fitness that was so encouraging but also the total support I had from my Matildas team-mates and the coaching staff.

Tony Gustavsson, who had replaced Ante Milicic, called me and insisted that the team and the organisation were going to support me through everything. They wanted me to succeed and for a woman elite athlete to be able to achieve her goals while being a mother.

CHAPTER TWENTY-TWO

Love in a Cold Climate

I've made some seemingly crazy decisions in my life but none has been as questionable as a single mother taking a six-month-old baby to the other side of the world to play football. But that's just what I did in 2022, not dreaming for a moment that it would turn out to be the best craziest decision I would ever make.

I didn't have any specific plans after the W-League finished so I asked one night at Brisbane Roar training if anyone knew of a European club that might be interested in having me for their domestic season.

Clare Polkinghorne, whom I'd followed to Norway two years before, mentioned that she'd re-signed with the Swedish team Vittsjo GIK after playing there the previous year.

Although they didn't have much money, she said there was a great family-friendly community at the club. 'They'd love to have you,' she insisted and put me in contact with the assistant coach, Thomas Martensson, who said he was happy to make a commitment to support me and Harper. He told the local media: 'Hiring a single parent who takes their daughter to a new country is, of course, a challenge and places demands on us as a club in many ways. But we have a good network of contacts around the club and we have many "nannies" who look forward to meeting both Katrina and her little Harper.'

Sweden has long been a leading team in women's football. The *Blagults*, meaning the Blue-Yellows, have twice won Olympic silver and have been runners-up and bronze medallists in the World Cup on several occasions, so their domestic competition, the Damallsvenskan League, is one of the best in the world.

To say that my mum was upset by my decision would be an understatement. In her own words she 'cried a lot', I suppose fearing that I was putting myself back into a vulnerable situation of being a long way from home without family support. Mum also knew that once I'd made up my mind, there was no way in the world that she could talk me out of it.

I was keenly aware of her concerns, but I was also certain it was no good sitting at home in Brisbane for several months with no football. I was not burnt out as I had been in 2018 and 2019, rather I was refreshed and eager to challenge myself and get my career back on track. I was not satisfied with being a bench player for the Matildas and wanted to show Tony Gustavsson that I could play a constructive role as a creative midfielder and be a major part of the 2023 World Cup.

Polks and I travelled over together after the Matildas' series against New Zealand in early April, but instead of arriving in Stockholm or Malmo, the club flew us into the northern city of Umea where the team was playing an away match.

Everything seemed to go wrong. First it was hard to get a taxi to take all our gear and then arrive at the team hotel to find that it didn't have reception and the computer system wasn't working properly. It wasn't the best first impression.

The next day we went to the match. Polks reluctantly agreed to play and went on in the second half as a substitute, but I was in no mood, jetlagged and with a baby on my lap and no nanny organised to help. There was a metre of snow on the ground and we had no warm clothes. Luckily Clara Markstedt, one of our new team-mates, had arranged some outfits worn by the baby of a friend of hers. So Harper was warm, but I was freezing my arse off as I sat on the benches and watched a terrible game that we lost 4–0.

I remember thinking to myself, 'What have I done?' It's one thing being a young, single woman on an adventure, as I had been on previous trips when I shared an apartment with a couple of team-mates and survived on food vouchers and my parents' generosity, but entirely another being a single mother with a baby wondering how to manage in a completely foreign environment.

I had 'met' Clara a month or so before when she WhatsApped me to say that she had been asked by Thomas to help me and Harper find an apartment and settle into our new lives in Sweden. She had been around the club for five or six years and enjoyed helping out the handful of internationals who came through each year.

Vittsjo is a lakeside town of barely 1600 people. The furniture giant IKEA had used the town's name to label a range of shelving. The football ground is Vittsjo's pride and joy, a 2000-seat stadium alongside an athletics track built behind the town. Other than that, the town centre is one street and not much more than a supermarket, car yard, flower store and a couple of pizzerias.

Most of the team actually lived in Kristianstad, a small city forty-five minutes south, which is where Clara had found a nice apartment for us, close to Polks and not far from her own place.

I chose the number 16 jersey because it was Harper's birthday and I slotted into the midfield when I took the field the next week in a home fixture against Djurgarden, a team from Stockholm, which we won.

This was a more pleasant start to an experience that I hoped would rejuvenate my international career but also confirm my sense that I could combine the role of mother and football on my own terms. Little did I know that it would provide so much more.

Over the next few weeks, as I settled into the side, we began to string together some good performances, with five wins and two draws in our next seven matches, including my first goal for the club. Clara scored three times in two matches, which helped leapfrog us up the table to third place.

She was a forward and a scoring mainstay of the club, as fit as anything and would back herself to be faster than any defender. We had an interesting beginning on the field because she liked having the ball delivered in behind where she could run onto the ball and score, but I also liked to sometimes deliver balls to the feet of the forwards and play one-two combinations as a variation, so it took a little while for us to understand how to work together.

I was seeing a lot of Clara off the field as well as she was helping me with necessities like a phone and how to find a legal car parking spot near my apartment. I would text her most nights so she could decipher where I was. I remember her being very patient but slightly irritated.

'You've sent me a photo of a tree and some random sign,' she would reply. 'How am I supposed to work out where you are?'

What I thought were signs with street names were actually parking instructions.

I really wasn't looking for love—I had too much on my plate with football and Harper, so I didn't notice the signs that she was attracted to me. Clara loved being around Harper, which I assumed was her motive for being around me. It was, in a way, but it was more that she admired me for the risk I had taken and how I managed things.

One night she asked me what I was up to and I told her I'd ordered Hello Fresh and was planning to make burgers for dinner. 'You can come over if you like,' I said, instantly regretting the offer because it meant I had to cook for two and entertain her.

Instead, she turned up with a bottle of wine and immediately took over the cooking while I looked after Harper. We had dinner and sat there talking about life. It was easy; she has this way about her that means you feel as if you can open up and share things without worrying. When she went home my feelings had changed and I thought I'd like to keep her around, even if it was just as friends.

I didn't know what I thought really. It was only when Mum came over for a visit in late May that my eyes were opened. 'She likes you,' was Mum's observation within a day or so. I dismissed the idea.

I had put my profile out on Tinder as a way of making new friends outside football, then Clara said to me one day: 'You keep popping up on my Tinder feed but you clearly haven't swiped me. It would be nice if you did, because then I could take you out on a date.'

I said something about not looking for a relationship but I still didn't get it. She would make little comments about a date and then, finally, I accepted. She worked in the city of Malmo most days. It was about an hour away so I got on the train one day with Harper and went down, got my nails done and did a bit of shopping before meeting her at a Japanese restaurant.

Mum called me in the middle of it and asked me what I was up to. I told her I was on a date with Clara.

'I told you,' Mum said. 'I knew there was something going on between you two.'

'Well I didn't know until just now,' I replied.

And that was that. I suddenly realised how I felt about Clara. She is such a calm person who is unfazed by life's ups and downs. I felt safe, excited and happy all at the same time. For me, that is love.

I introduced Clara to the world in mid-July, with a photo of us frying potatoes during a barbecue on the island of Gotland, off Sweden's east coast where she grew up. 'Gotland stole my heart,' I wrote, but I was really referring to Clara. I was smitten, convinced I had finally found a partner in life. Clara also posted, not a photo of us but me and Harper relaxing in a hammock, laughing. 'My happy pills,' she wrote simply.

My personal life may have been on the up, but out on the field the Matildas were struggling. An early exit from the Asian Cup in January—beaten by South Korea in the quarter-finals—had set the tone for the year, and by the time the team arrived in Europe in June for two matches, we had slumped to twelfth in the FIFA rankings.

I joined the team (Clara came along as well), which was scheduled to play Spain and then Portugal, for which Tony Gustavsson had brought over a fresh-faced squad, given that senior players like Sam Kerr, Steph Catley, Caitlin Foord and Hayley Raso couldn't make the trip.

He called it 'a crucial period of groundwork', experimenting with a squad of younger players and team formations. Even so, he wasn't expecting a 7–0 thrashing by Spain in what was statistically the worst performance of an Australian team in more than twenty-five years.

It was a rout, plain and simple, and could have been worse, believe it or not, as they had twenty-three shots on goal while we managed just four, although the story was much more complex.

I played the first half, during which we held out against the home team for all but the last minute when they scored through a wonderful strike by midfielder Aitana Bonmati, who would go on to win the FIFA Ballon d'Or for the best women's player during the season.

The second half was a different story as I sat on the bench with other senior players while Tony rotated players and positions, giving younger squad members the chance to play against the sixth-ranked side in the world. Grilled afterwards, Tony insisted that he had experimented because he wanted answers. 'It's about the long term, 2023 and beyond,' he said, adding that the result was a 'wake-up call for a lot of people'.

It was a much better performance three days later against Portugal where we held a 1–0 advantage until the last two minutes of the game when the Portuguese clawed back a controversial equaliser. On a personal note, I was pleased to play a role in our goal, finding Larissa Crummer from halfway with a through ball that she crossed to allow Princess Ibini-Isei to score her maiden international goal.

On the surface, the results looked bad, with the World Cup less than a year away, but it was clear that experimentation and blooding young players was part of building a team and perfecting tactics. And history would show that Tony, who was under intense pressure at the time, would be proved right in his squad development.

And I was front and centre in his experiments.

In a strange way, my early international goal-scoring success between 2014 and 2017 seemed to have caused me selection problems in the years to come as national coaches and team tactics changed.

My role as a midfield creator had slowly changed, and instead I was used more as an attacking player and a regular contributor on the score sheet. But as the goals dried up and my form dipped during my down periods through 2018 to 2020, so too did my selection options. Staj and then Ante struggled to find a place for me in their structure. I don't blame them, given my problems.

Tony changed all that, moving me into a deep midfield role—number 6—where my ball control, running and passing once again became my most important assets rather than my thirty-metre strikes. I revelled in the job—the *regista*, the creative playmaker and the link between defence and attack that helped retain possession and create the chances for others.

I was the team quarterback, according to Tony's description. 'We want to dominate the games with the ball, to penetrate and break lines and attack. You need a No. 6 who can be that quarterback and that engine and heart of the team.'

The Matildas had slipped to thirteenth in the FIFA rankings by September when I returned to Australia to join the team for two matches against Canada. Our performances may have been patchy, with just eight wins from our last twenty-four matches, but our fan base had continued to grow. More than 25,000 people turned up at Lang Park in Brisbane to watch the first game on 3 September 2022.

We were always going to struggle against the reigning Olympic champions, particularly with seven of our key players missing, including Steph Catley, Caitlin Foord and Ellie Carpenter, but it was made more difficult when Canadian winger Adriana Leon scored in the eleventh minute.

From then on it was a case of missed opportunities and some great goalkeeping that denied us an equaliser.

I had another good game, although I was still coming to terms with finding a balance between defensive and attacking work, as I told the media after the match.

'Sometimes I get too eager to get a bit too far forward and not balance the team properly. But the more us midfielders can get on the ball, the more control we usually have of the game. I'm still learning and building, but coming up against a team like Canada, playing a bit of a different formation, I've got to find spaces on the field and I think that's something I can definitely work on. Most of the play usually goes through the No. 6 and through our midfield, and because we do have such a strong attacking force we do create a lot of chances. I think that's where we can do better.'

The crowd was even bigger in Sydney three nights later with almost 27,000 people. The match at Allianz Stadium couldn't have begun better when, in the third minute, Sam Kerr found Mary Fowler with a cutback pass and she calmly slotted it home. Our attacks continued through the first half as we controlled possession and looked a much better side while Canada found it difficult to create any real chances.

But everything changed in the second half as Canada put us under more pressure and Leon again cut us to ribbons. She scored twice in five minutes to give Canada the lead, which they held to win 2–1.

Tony conceded that we were running out of time. There were just forty-six days of what he called 'FIFA windows' before the World Cup. When you took out fourteen travel and recovery days, it left us with thirty-two days of which twenty-two would be taken up with matches and pre-game sessions: 'That leaves us with ten proper training sessions where we can work out all the details,' he told the media, adding: 'When you believe, it means you can achieve something . . . and I believe in this team and the process.'

The Matildas returned to Europe in October for two more matches, the first a 'home' match against South Africa in London followed by a trip to the Danish city of Viborg for a clash with Denmark.

We were in need of a morale booster after the series loss to Canada and even though the African champions were modest opposition, the 4–1 win provided the result we were hoping for before facing a much sterner test against the Danes, whom we had never beaten.

It wasn't a great start to our match against Denmark, conceding a goal in just forty-seven seconds, according to the official timer, as we got tangled up in defence.

But we slowly began to gain control over the game, even though we went into the half-time break still a goal behind. The opportunities kept coming early in the second half but it wasn't until the sixty-sixth minute that we got the equaliser when Caitlin Foord scored with a deflected shot.

At 1–1 our tails were up and just five minutes later I got a chance at some personal glory when the ball came free five metres outside the top of the box. My eyes lit up as I took one step and launched into a strike that beat the goalkeeper and buried the ball in the back of the net.

'A wonder goal from the wonder mum,' the television commentator called as the cameras showed Tony Gustavsson fist-pumping the air. The goal was reminiscent of my form back in 2014. The match was settled a few minutes later when Kyra Cooney-Cross made a driving forward run and found Caitlin in the centre who turned and shot over the keeper's head to make it three goals in just nine minutes.

I have never defined myself by my goal-scoring, but I felt the exhilaration of scoring my first international goal as a mum—proof that I still had the ability to be a valuable goal-scoring member of the Matildas. The win would also prove to be important psychologically for the World Cup that was now just nine months away.

In between these international matches, I still had playing commitments back at Vittsjo. The Swedish Damallsvenskan League was coming to a close after almost eight months. Clara had enjoyed a productive season with eight goals while I had played in twenty-two fixtures and scored three times as well as making several assists, including Clara's last goal of the season on 5 November.

A week later, with Clara beside me, I was back in Australia as the Matildas faced one last significant challenge for the season—Sweden. It was rather funny when you think about it; me on the plane with my Swedish girlfriend about to play against her national team. Who would she barrack for, I challenged her. 'You, of course,' she replied. 'And Sweden.'

If the 22,000 fans who flocked into AAMI Park in Melbourne had only seen the first thirty minutes of the match then they would have left disappointed. The *Blagults* led us a merry dance and threatened to establish an early lead that would have been hard to overcome, but sometimes a tactical change can work wonders.

Sweden had dominated the midfield early so we changed systems to a format in which Kyra Cooney-Cross and I acted as box-to-box midfielders while Hayley Raso and Cortnee Vine pushed wider and Caitlin Foord moved closer to Sam Kerr upfront to add some extra firepower.

The changes paid dividends almost immediately. Just before half-time I began a chain of passes that led to Sam Kerr scoring with a toe poke on the near post and we went into the break with an unlikely lead.

We opened up in the second half with Caitlin curling one past the Swedish keeper after a fantastic solo run to make it 2–0. Ten minutes later, we had a third when I made a long crossfield pass out of defence to Sam, who cleverly found Mary Fowler in the middle. Caitlin then got her second to put icing on the cake and give us our biggest win over the Swedes. More importantly, we had a brand-new strategy for physical, attacking football.

We continued in similar style three nights later in Newcastle against Thailand although we struggled to get the ball in the net with three strikes hitting the crossbar. The breakthrough came when I delivered an in-swinging corner which Sam leaped for to nod into the net. The lead was doubled soon after half-time when Hayley Raso and Emily van Egmond, back in the side after almost two years, combined in a delightful one-two with Hayley beating the keeper. We cruised to victory 2–0 but rued our missed chances—we had twenty-eight shots on goal compared to Thailand's three.

How things had changed. Barely two months before we were being written off as World Cup contenders after losing to Canada at home, and now we had beaten two of our biggest opponents, Denmark and Sweden. I had settled into the number 6 role and completed my post-pregnancy comeback.

A few days later I posted on Instagram a team photo taken on the ground after the game against Sweden. I beamed in the front row, with Harper perched on my knee wearing a tiny Australia shirt. The caption summed up the moment:

> Surrounded by so many inspiring women, in a stadium filled with screaming Aussie fans. These are the photos that I can't wait to show Harper when she's older. forever grateful

Christmas 2022 was a particularly sweet celebration for me, home after an amazing overseas experience with Harper and in love with a woman with whom I could see myself spending the rest of my life.

CHAPTER TWENTY-THREE

No, I Mean Yes

If you need some extra matches to sharpen up your game before a major tournament then the solution is simple—create one of your own.

Australia had hosted a 'Cup of Nations' in the lead-up to the 2019 World Cup in France, inviting New Zealand, South Korea and Argentina to compete in a round-robin series similar to the Algarve Cup. The tournament was played in Sydney, Melbourne and Brisbane. We won our three matches, and the Cup, comfortably.

The tournament was revived in February 2023 for the same reason. This time it not only gave us solid match practice against two decent sides, the Czech Republic and Jamaica, but more importantly, it pitted us against Spain, who had recently beaten the USA and would be one of our biggest opponents if we were going to make an impression at the World Cup.

There are two ways to look at our performance against the Czech Republic, the first match played at Gosford on the Central Coast. If you take the negative viewpoint then our first half against the twenty-eighth ranked side in the world was disappointing as we were held goal-less despite a number of chances. But if you consider that the Czechs had held both Great Britain and the USA to goal-less draws during 2022 then the performance seems much better.

The second half was a complete contrast as the floodgates opened and we scored four unanswered goals, including a brace to Hayley Raso, and singles to Sam Kerr and Clare Polkinghorne. It was a solid start to the tournament. Spain had beaten Jamaica 3–0 in the earlier match which gave us a yardstick about scoring, given that the tournament could be decided on goal difference.

We played the key game against Spain three days later in a double-header at the Commonwealth Bank Stadium in Sydney. Unlike our match against the Czech Republic, our first half was electric. Cortnee Vine scored within ten minutes and Clare Polkinghorne added a second just five minutes later.

We had Spain on the back foot as more chances went begging, Sam Kerr was denied a goal with an incorrect offside call before Caitlin Foord made it 3–0 just before half-time.

But the second half slowed as Spain fought back. Even though the scoreline finished 3–2, the Spanish goals from

Olga Carmona and Alba Redondo Ferrer were both late and we got our redemption for the 7–0 thrashing the same side had given us just eight months before. Looking back, and perhaps strangely given all the big games I've played over the years, this win was one of the most memorable simply because it showed the spirit of the Matildas and how well we combined when up against the best teams.

At the post-match media conference Tony Gustavsson downplayed the first-half display although noting that we had become a much more dynamic attacking side since the European summer. He was more excited by the second half, and how we were able to corral Spain for long periods. The late goals were disappointing but did not take away from the performance, he insisted.

'We will always have more goal-scoring chances than our opponents but we must be able to defend against a team like Spain who are so freaking good on the ball. What I'm most proud of is that they were a team out there tonight. We attacked in one formation and defended in another, and that takes time and training.'

Tony said the victory was the result the team needed to confirm a belief that the development was worth the effort: 'It will give us the confidence that we need to know that it was all worth it.'

We needed only a draw against Jamaica on the last day to win the tournament but a solid win was our aim as the caravan moved back up the coast to Newcastle.

My game began in a crazy fashion when I got tangled up with Jamaican midfielder Drew Spence and was fouled as she lashed out with her foot after the whistle had gone. I leaped up, and considered retaliating for a split second before deciding to express my frustration to the referee.

As usual, my language was a little strong and I copped a yellow card as well. Dad, who was watching on from the stands, gave me a tongue-lashing after the game for being so ill-disciplined.

But I had the last laugh when, just a minute later, Caitlin Foord found me with a great pass. I was in space just outside the box and I let fly with a curling shot that beat the keeper into the right-hand netting.

I whooped and hollered as I ran up the ground, skipping because our assistant coach had told me to fly like an eagle if I scored. The television commentator laughed: 'That's a Katrina Gorry special. She's been fired up for this one since the opening minutes and she's fired the Matildas in front.'

I had a hand in our second goal too, with an assist to Alex Chidiac early in the second half before Caitlin banged home a long-range strike of her own as we cruised home to win 3–0. Spain beat the Czech Republic 3–0 in the other, earlier game but we had won the tournament, which Tony insisted was an important aspect in the lead-up to the World Cup.

'We haven't played tournament football for a long time so, in that sense, it was very important. We learned what it feels like to win.'

I was back in Sweden by mid-March, having played most of the Aussie domestic season with Brisbane 'on loan' from Vittsjo, which was now preparing for the new Damallsvenskan season.

The Roar was now a young side, filled with potential rather than the one I joined a decade before that had half the Matildas in its squad. In 2023 there was only me and Larissa Crummer, which shows how much women's football has changed in that time as more and more experienced players head off overseas to play in Europe and the US where the seasons are longer, the standard of competition better and the contracts more lucrative.

The rest of the Matildas squad arrived in London a few weeks later for two friendlies to help round out our World Cup preparations. It might seem like a rush to travel halfway around the world to play just two games but we only have time for a couple of ten-day camps each year to fit in with the various European domestic competitions.

Sometimes nothing seems to go right. The Matildas had one of those days on 7 April when we met a very resolute

Scottish side in a friendly played at Wimbledon in front of several thousand spectators.

The match marked the return of Ellie Carpenter after a two-year break while Tony rested several experienced players, including Sam Kerr, Steph Catley and Caitlin Foord.

We expected to win, given our recent good form and Scotland's FIFA ranking (24), but we also knew that Scotland was a more than capable side, and quite a physical one, so the match would be a good test.

We opened brightly enough with several chances in the first half, two of which cannoned off the woodwork. None had found the net as we left the field at half-time, frustrated at 0–0.

The problem with failing to score is that your misfortune is highlighted when the other team finds the net, which is exactly what the Scots did early in the second half when defender Nicola Docherty produced a looping strike from the left edge of the box which carried over Mackenzie Arnold's outstretched hands and found the top far corner of the net. It was a freak shot and Scotland, who were playing a very physical game, were ahead 1–0.

The goal brought us to life but our poor luck continued with another shot, a strike by Clare Hunt from twenty metres, again hitting the woodwork. In all, we had seventeen shots on goal for no return as Scotland celebrated victory.

It was a jolt to our preparations, our first loss in seven matches.

England had been unbeaten for thirty matches when we faced them four days later at Brentford in West London. The Lionesses were riding high as European champions and had just beaten Brazil in front of 83,000 fans at Wembley Stadium to win the UEFA Women's Finalissima, the playoff between the European champions and the equivalent South American tournament, the Copa America.

The first half of our match against them was relatively quiet until the thirty-second minute when England's defence made an error by playing the ball half-heartedly back to the keeper, Mary Earps. Sam Kerr, back in the team, pounced and chipped the ball over the head of the stranded keeper to give us a 1–0 lead.

Sam turned from scorer to provider early in the second half when she ran onto a through ball on the right wing before crossing into the middle where Charli Grant headed it past Earps to give us a 2–0 lead. It was Charli's first goal for the Matildas and we celebrated wildly before collecting ourselves and staving off any English comeback.

Tony summed up our change of fortune after the game: 'It was our execution [in front of goal] tonight. It was brilliant. England has a lot of weapons; they can play through you, around you and over you. They have a lot of combinations and if you don't play as a team then you get exposed.

'We have to stay humble at this stage [leading up to the World Cup]. Sometimes you are not as good as people say you are when you win, and sometimes, like against Scotland, you are not as bad as they say when you lose.'

The win was a morale booster after the Scotland loss and an important yardstick against an opponent we were likely to encounter in the knockout stage of the World Cup. Of course, a friendly is vastly different from the pressures of a World Cup encounter and England was quick to play down the significance of the match. The warning signs were there, particularly their dominance in possession through the game, that if we met on the pitch at the World Cup in August then the result could be very different.

I made it clear to Clara early on in our relationship that I would never propose to her. It wasn't that I was ruling out marriage entirely, it was just that I couldn't bring myself to initiate something that could have consequences for myself and Harper if it all went wrong.

There was something inside me, some nagging, irritating piece of sand in my shoe that made me question whether love could ever last. In my relationships over the years, there had always been some aspect about the other person or our compatibility that I papered over and tried to ignore, which ultimately convinced me that nothing was permanent.

But Clara was different, and I knew deep down, even after a few months, that she was my person—The One.

I had asked her to be my girlfriend by writing a message on Harper's singlet which read *Please will you be my mum's girlfriend*, so I figured that I had done my bit.

Within a couple of weeks of getting together we decided to test living under the same roof. Clara ran a business from home when she wasn't in Malmo, so I knew that me being there all the time would make a big difference, not to mention having a seven-month-old roaming around the flat, demanding attention and terrorising everything.

My fear was that things would be too complicated, but I was wrong, and when the trial period of a month was up I bought a coffee machine and a Dyson vacuum cleaner, so she knew that I wasn't leaving. And also because she probably wouldn't kick me out as they were two things that we used every day. It was my buy-in to the relationship.

Life with Clara just felt really easy from the start. It didn't matter what we were doing, whether it was going to training or cooking dinner, or going to the park. It all seemed effortless. I guess that's why things progressed so quickly.

I can be quite stubborn and there are times I just want to sit on my own. When that happens, Clara understands and gives me space for a while before she comes in and sits quietly beside me on the couch. Somehow she is able to draw me out of myself and chat through things. To make things better again.

So here I was in a relationship that I didn't believe existed, wanting to be with this woman forever but letting my own misgivings stop me from doing anything about it. Clara solved it all by proposing to me.

I hate surprises—not the outcome itself but the secrecy that surrounds them—so I was uneasy when Clara started talking about celebrating our first anniversary of being a couple. I became more suspicious when my Matildas team-mate Charli Grant, who had joined Vittsjo that season, turned up one day to go shopping with me but, instead, decided to stay with Clara because they had 'something to do'. I went off in a huff.

A few weeks before our anniversary—11 June—Clara announced that she had arranged for us to go away for the night—alone—to celebrate. Charli and Teagan Micah, another Matildas team-mate who was playing for Rosengard, had agreed to take care of Harper while we were away. I couldn't really refuse even though I was now convinced that something was afoot.

Clara was taking me to the seaside town of Falkenberg, a special place for her near to her grandparents where she had spent many happy childhood summers. We arrived in the afternoon and had a swim before having a picnic with a couple of drinks while listening to our favourite music. It was very chill and I began to relax until Clara suddenly presented me with a twenty-minute video on her iPad that she had made (with Charli's help that afternoon) about our first year together.

I was blown away and had tears in my eyes at the gesture and the realisation of how wonderfully magic the year had been. When the video finished I turned around to hug her to find that she was on one knee offering me a ring and proposing.

My instinctive response was regrettable: 'Nooo.' I choked on the word, realising in that moment that it was shock rather than an answer. 'Yes,' I blurted out, trying to make up for my mistake. 'This is crazy but yes, of course.'

Despite my reservations, when the moment came I knew it was exactly what I wanted and I could not have wished for a more loving and romantic way to be asked. The rest of the afternoon was surreal, a world on our own in the midst of nature at its most beautiful.

Later that day we both posted about it on Instagram with a series of photographs of us at the beach and in hotel bathrobes, kissing and showing off our matching diamond engagement rings. Clara was relieved that her amazing proposal had worked:

> She said YES! 💍 How did I get so lucky?

I also posted:

> The best love stories never end. YES

The posts were liked 32,000 times.

If that wasn't romantic enough, we went to her grandmother's house the next day because Clara wanted to explain the rings. There is a tradition in Sweden in which the person buying the ring to propose must buy one of their own. Clara's grandmother, Annette, had offered her fiftieth and sixtieth birthday rings but Clara insisted on buying them rather than accepting them as a gift.

She had then taken the rings to a Gotland Island jeweller to have the diamonds reset and the rings refashioned. Her parents, Susanne and Peter, had accompanied her to the jewellers where they celebrated with happy photos and champagne toasts.

When we left for Australia a month or so later, the conversation was not just about the excitement of the upcoming World Cup. Clara and I were also making plans for an addition to our little family—another baby.

CHAPTER TWENTY-FOUR

World Cup Mania

Even now I can't quite believe the Australian public's response to the World Cup. On the eve of the tournament it was announced that more than 1.4 million tickets had been presold, meaning it was a financial success before kick-off.

Incredibly, all five matches to be played at Sydney's Stadium Australia, a stadium with a capacity of almost 76,000 spectators, were sold out. It was mind-boggling to see those numbers as we made final preparations for the first match against Ireland on 20 July in Sydney.

Tony Gustavsson had described our group draw as tough. Canada was the obvious problem, having beaten us twice in Australia the previous year, but Ireland and Nigeria both presented stumbling blocks if we were going to progress from the group stage and have a chance of winning knockout matches.

The Irish coach Vera Pauw admitted that, although Ireland had beaten us 3–2 in Dublin back in 2021, Australia was the better side. 'But somehow we managed to win,' she observed about the earlier game. It was an important message because in tournament play it's all about finding a way to win the game; adapting to the moment to win. The other big message was that anything can happen; don't expect a result, make it happen.

We had to deal with the last-minute withdrawal of our captain Sam Kerr because of a calf strain she suffered in a training mishap three days before. It was a huge setback for us, not just because of her abilities on the pitch but the psychology of her absence. Wasn't fortune supposed to smile on us as hosts? Apparently not.

If Ireland were nervous then we were doubly so as we ran out into the arena in front of a capacity crowd of 75,784. The roar from so many people creates a sound wave that you can feel physically, a sort of surreal white noise that somehow fills the space around you. Your body is on autopilot; movements happen without thought, so naturally that you feel untouchable.

The opening to the game was understandably tense and we struggled to impose ourselves as Ireland adopted a tactic of sitting back to soak up the pressure and wait for a chance on the counter-attack. Their defensive plan worked as, even though we dominated possession, we went into the half-time break 0–0.

Our chance to get on the scoreboard finally came five minutes into the second half when Hayley Raso was bundled over in the box by an over-enthusiastic Irish defender and the referee waved away Irish protests and awarded a penalty.

Steph Catley, who was standing in as captain in Sam's absence, stepped up to take the kick. The rest of us held our breath as she paused for a moment before slamming the ball into the top left-hand side of the net. Steph raced off up the field in joy as we celebrated with the crowd at the halfway line. It was a relief that we were up and running in the tournament.

From then on we began to grow and held sway for the rest of the game, although an increasingly desperate Ireland forced a few chances during the six minutes of injury time and produced several nervous moments, including an Irish free kick being deflected onto the roof of the net. But we held on to get an uninspiring but valuable win to begin the tournament.

I was happy with my form, and even fired off a couple of shots at goal, but we knew that we had to improve if we were going to make an impact. Tony admitted that we'd had to change our tactics because of the loss of Sam.

'This wasn't the fantastic attacking Australian team we see when the Matildas are flying,' he said. 'It was a team that finds a way to win a game and does what's needed in that moment. I've been around tournament football long enough to know that sometimes it's those games where you just need to grind through and find a way to win them, and that showed some maturity in this team.'

Unbeknown to me there was a row brewing over a comment made during the match by Channel Seven television commentator David Basheer who had been impressed by a tackle I had made.

'Certainly motherhood has not blunted her competitive instincts, that's for sure,' he said. 'She is one fighter for Australia.'

The notion that motherhood could somehow blunt instincts enraged hundreds of viewers, but I saw it as clumsy rather than insulting. I was questioned about it the morning after the Ireland game.

'I don't take things like that too personally,' I said. 'I don't look at it as a negative comment, but can see how it got taken the wrong way. I'm sure he didn't mean it in a negative way, sometimes things just come out the wrong way.'

The comments were actually a positive because they highlighted publicly my personal battle to get back into the side as a mum, but also the support I'd had from family and friends. There was also the unexpected bonus of seeing the effect of Harper's presence in the change rooms.

'Having Harper in camp with us has been amazing,' I said. 'She brings light to the end of a tough day and makes everything happy. The girls love her too because it breaks up football mode and makes it feel like a family.'

Our next match against Nigeria would be extra special because it would be in Brisbane. 'I promised myself after Harper's birth that I would do everything I could to get into the side to play this World Cup and now to play in front of a home crowd is a dream come true and helps repay my family for all their support and sacrifices along the way.'

But, as I would learn, fairytales don't always end well.

—

If we needed reminding that tournament football is different from the normal round of friendlies and minor cups that we play each year, then Nigeria's match with Canada the following night showed that we could take nothing for granted.

Canada, the Olympic champions, were expected to comfortably account for the African champions, whose FIFA ranking was just forty-five, but instead it was the Super Falcons who showed mettle to absorb periods of Canadian dominance and deny what seemed inevitable goals. The 0–0 draw threw open all sorts of possibilities and made our match with Nigeria even more important.

Things didn't start well as Mary Fowler had joined Sam Kerr on the injured list and, yet again, we had to rejig our attacking tactics to accommodate the loss of two of our best scorers. Still, we settled into the match quite well and looked dangerous, using long diagonal balls to set up forays into attack, racking up eight corners in the first half alone.

But Nigeria carried on from their form against Canada with some stoic defence and, despite several good chances, we were into injury time in the first half before the breakthrough happened.

I latched onto a goal kick from the Nigerian goalkeeper that had fallen short of halfway and managed to make an off-balanced first-time pass to Caitlin Foord who was sprinting down the left wing. Caitlin looked up to see Emily van Egmond running into the top of the box and made a wonderfully weighted pass that allowed Emily to slot it home.

But the capacity crowd's joy at our lead was hushed just three minutes later when, on the cusp of half-time, a scuffed and deflected cross by Nigeria cannoned luckily to forward Uchenna Kanu who managed to turn the ball into the net. For all our work, we were 1–1 at the break.

The second half continued in much the same way. I fired off a shot from the edge of the box but watched it sail just over the crossbar and then got tangled up in a collision with midfielder Toni Payne who hobbled off injured.

Nigeria won a corner in the sixty-fourth minute and when we failed to properly clear our lines, and after a series of headers in the box, centre back Osinachi Ohale charged through to nod the ball into the net to give Nigeria the lead. It was 2–1.

Disaster struck in the seventy-first minute when there was a defensive mix-up as Alanna Kennedy tried to play the ball back to Mackenzie Arnold only to have Nigeria's star striker

Asisat Oshoala anticipate the move, pounce on the loose ball and finish from a tight angle to make it 3–1 with less than twenty minutes to play.

Suddenly, we were in very real danger of not making it to the knockout rounds. Eleven minutes of injury time gave us hope but we simply could not finish in front of goal. First it was Alex Chidiac who fired over the crossbar, then Kyra Cooney-Cross overhit a corner, and Caitlin Foord couldn't get her header past the keeper in a one-on-one contest.

With barely two minutes on the clock, Alanna Kennedy made amends for the earlier mix-up by rising high above the Nigerian defence at the back post to power home a goal and give us a faint sniff of rescuing the match. There was one last chance as Alex hit a long pass to Alanna who knocked it to the feet of Ellie Carpenter only to have her shot saved by a desperate keeper.

We'd had sixty-four per cent possession during the game and fired off seventeen shots on goal compared to Nigeria's six shots and yet we'd lost 3–2 when the final whistle sounded.

I didn't feel much like talking to the media after the game but it was my turn, and I was determined to stay positive: 'It's obviously disappointing but I still think we created a lot of chances,' I told the media. 'We kept possession of the ball well, so there were some positives to take out of the game. We've got to recover and be prepared for Canada. We both need to win. We know we are good when our backs are against the wall. We believe in ourselves and know we have the home crowd advantage.'

—

What a night it was! With everything on the line, including the potential of an embarrassing early exit from our own tournament, the Matildas responded with one of our most complete performances since I joined the team.

There are days when everything goes wrong and you can't get the ball in the net, but on this night in front of 27,000 people at AAMI Park in Melbourne, it seemed we could hardly miss, from the moment we ran out onto the ground under a full moon to the sounds of the INXS classic 'New Sensation'. The only downer was that Sam Kerr would start on the bench, uncertain still if she would be able to play.

We were very aware that this was the biggest match in the Matildas' forty-five-year history, with the weight of not only our own self-belief but national expectations on our shoulders. Not only was the stadium full but 2.4 million Australians watched the game on television that night, a record for women's sport.

It took just nine minutes for us to get on the scoreboard when Steph Catley, standing in as captain again, made a run down the left wing and crossed into the top of the box. The bouncing ball escaped the Canadian defence and fell for Hayley Raso, who took two touches, picked her target and struck it home into the left-hand netting. Our celebrations were silenced by the lineswoman raising an offside flag but a VAR review dismissed the ruling and Hayley's goal stood. The grateful crowd got to celebrate a second time.

VAR intervened again soon afterwards when Ellie Carpenter was controversially ruled offside after a passage of play during which Mary Fowler jumped onto a loose ball and lashed it into the net.

But justice was restored a few minutes later when a corner kick taken by Kyra Cooney-Cross eluded the Canadian goal-keeper and bounced around the goal line, falling to the feet of Hayley who instinctively swivelled and stuck the ball in the net in a single motion.

It was 2–0 and the stadium erupted again as we played out the last few minutes of the half to protect our lead while Tony Gustavsson earned a yellow card for his excitement on the sideline.

Ours was a solid lead but we knew that we could not relax against the Olympic champions, who were also fighting for tournament survival. The Canadians made four substitutions at half-time in the hope of turning around their fortunes.

Tony was buoyant, insisting that we should keep the attacking pressure rather than sit back and defend our lead. And the tactic paid off just ten minutes into the second half when Caitlin Foord, deep on the left-hand side, got a cross into the box where Mary Fowler, wearing black gloves in the winter cold, got a touch on the ball as it rolled into the goal.

Now it was 3–0 and the crowd was delirious. We could hardly hear each other in the middle of the ground as we tried to stay calm and stick to the game plan. It was tempting now to sit back and defend but Canada were beaten as we pushed forward again with Mary just missing a second goal when her powerful drive struck the right-hand upright.

There was one last hurrah when I was fouled just inside the box with only minutes to go and Steph slotted in our fourth goal from the penalty spot. 'It's the cherry on the top,' the television commentator crowed as we swamped Steph on the sideline, knowing we had triumphed at the point of disaster.

Instead, it was Canada who exited after a goal-less draw between Nigeria and Ireland meant we had topped the pool. Our opponents in the first knockout game would be Denmark, and we were now a team to be reckoned with—hopefully with a fit Sam Kerr.

Playing for Mansfield Eagles in the local church league at age ten. The club did not have a girls' team, so I had to play with the boys. It made no difference to me. I was used to playing with my brothers.

Dad and Michelle's wedding in 2002. They had to push the wedding back a few hours because I was playing a football game! Back (*left to right*): Amanda, Michelle, Dad (Peter). Front: Lachlan, Me, Eden, Daniel and Joel.

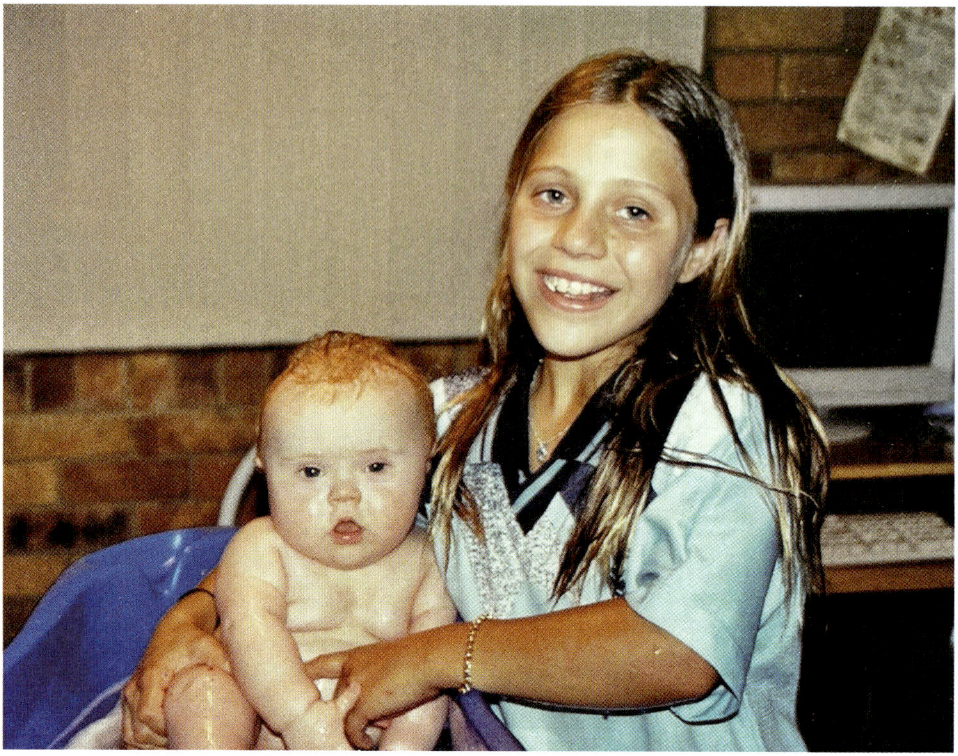

Age eleven, bathing my brother Dylan. I loved mothering him.

My best friend, Jade Saunders, and me. We were probably about twelve here. Everyone thought we were twins.

Daniel, Lachlan, me, Eden and Joel camping at Double Island Point near Noosa.

With my dad, Peter, at the 2014 Asian Football Confederation awards in Manila. I was named Women's Player of the Year.

With my roomie Michelle Heyman at the 2016 Rio Olympics.

After my last game in Japan my Mynavi Sendai teammates threw me up in the air! *Mynavi Sendai*

With our squad and supporters. The freshness of my experience in Japan was a blessing for me. I loved spending time in this amazing country and learning more about its society and values, not to mention the lure of the skills and playing style of Japanese football. *Mynavi Sendai*

Playing for Brisbane Roar against Melbourne City in our premiership-winning season 2017–18. My secret weapon, even from a young age, has been tackling. I've always loved the slide tackle, sweeping the ball from beneath the feet of my opponents and watching the surprise on their faces, as well as the faces of the opposition coaches. *Albert Perez/ZUMA Wire/Alamy*

My stepmum Michelle, brother Dylan and Dad after the Matildas beat Thailand 6–0 in a 2020 Olympic qualifier in Sydney. Dad and Michelle have driven to my matches all around Australia, first when I was playing in junior teams and then in my early years playing in the W-League with Melbourne Victory and Adelaide United, and later with Brisbane Roar and the Matildas.

A family photo at Harper's Gender Reveal in 2021. Back (*left to right*): Dad, Michelle, Samantha, Eden, Mum, David, me, Amanda, Lachlan. Front: Joel, Amira-Lee, Dylan, Rio (our puppy), Justin holding Brooklyn, and Remii.

My beautiful sister Amanda has always been there to guide me through life's challenges and the extraordinary moments. She was next to me when I gave birth to Harper and is someone who constantly inspires me.

With Dad and Harper just after her birth on 16 August 2021.

With my mum, Linda, and Harper in Melbourne in 2021 after scoring in Brisbane's win over Melbourne Victory. During my first season after Harper's birth Mum travelled around with me to take care of her while I was playing and training.

11 June 2023. Falkenberg, Sweden, a special place for Clara where she had spent many happy childhood summers. We arrived in the afternoon and had a swim before a picnic, then Clara was on one knee offering me a ring and proposing.

Fathers Day 2023: Samuel, Pop (Kevin), Joel, Dylan, Lachlan, Ben, Hannah and me.

With my support crew at the 2023 World Cup in Australia: (*back*) Lachlan, Dylan, Michelle, Dad, Clara, David, (*front*) Tim, Remii, me, Harper and Mum.

The penalty shootout win against France in the 2023 World Cup quarter-final, the longest shootout in World Cup history. I had erased the Brazil penalty regrets from my mind. I waited for the whistle and struck the ball as hard as possible, then watched as the keeper, Solene Durand, moved the same way. She got her hands into the path of the ball but it burst through and into the net. *A.B. Ratnayake/Reuters/AAP*

Lining up for the Matildas in front of 75,000 fans before the 2023 World Cup semi-final against England at Stadium Australia: (*clockwise*) Ellie Carpenter, Kyra Cooney-Cross, Mary Fowler, Clare Hunt, Mackenzie Arnold, Clare Polkinghorn, me, Caitlin Foord, Sam Kerr, Steph Catley and Hayley Raso. *Isabel Infantes/PA/Alamy*

The maternity shoot before Koby was born. *Megan Ewens*

Cuddling Koby in hospital after he was born on 9 June 2024.

Harper meeting her little brother Koby for the first time.

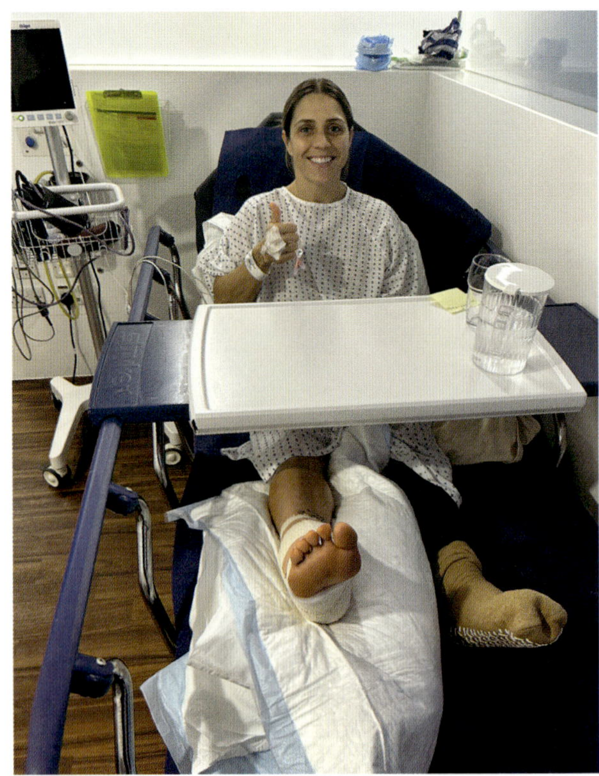

Following ankle surgery in 2024 after my injury against Chelsea for West Ham.

Travelling with Harper and Koby to the Paris Olympics in 2024.
Ann Odong

Back in Australia for Koby's first Christmas in 2024. In Brisbane with (*top row*) Eden, Karen, Tim, Clara, Daniel, Amanda, Brooklyn, Justin, Michelle, Peter, Dylan, Luna, Lachlan, Remii, Leo (Lachlan's dog), Mum, David, (*bottom row*) Amira-Lee, me with Koby and Harper, Levi, Jessiah, Joel and Samantha.

Me, Joel and Amira-Lee on Christmas Day, 2024. I learnt my toughness on the football field playing against Joel, and he and I are now both in a much better place with the help of our incredible family.

Playing at home for West Ham against Liverpool in the Women's Super League. I immediately felt at home at West Ham, and the women's game is growing rapidly in the UK, where fans live and breathe club football.
Pedro Porru/SPP/Alamy

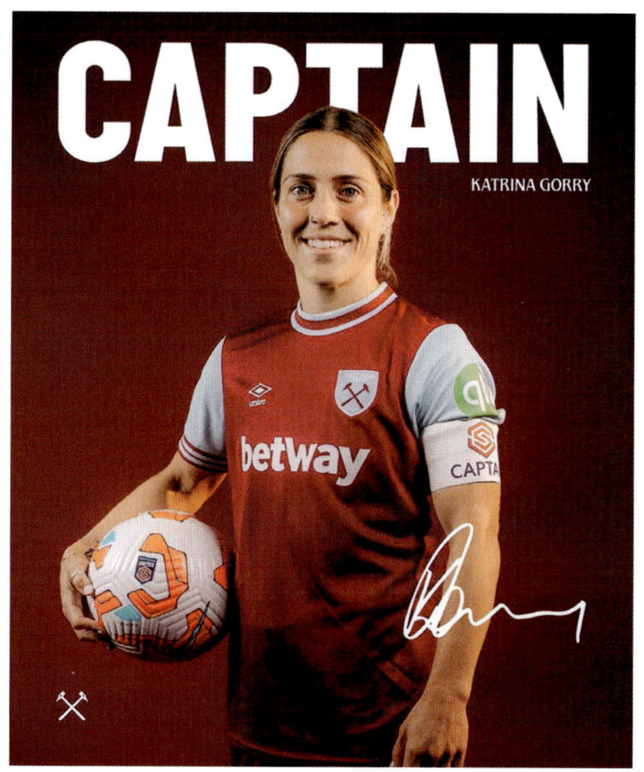

Taking on a new role as captain of West Ham United. It was the first time in my career that I had been asked to lead. I understand why people talk about it being an honour. I couldn't stop grinning as I put on the armband.
West Ham United

My No. 1 supporters!
West Ham United

Having a kickaround with Harper near our home in England.
Jack Lawson Photo

My family—the most important team of all! *Jack Lawson Photo*

CHAPTER TWENTY-FIVE

Redemption

The audience numbers and public anticipation just kept rising as we lined up against Denmark seven days later at Stadium Australia where another 75,000-plus crowd thundered their approval and a peak audience of 3.75 million watched on television and online, the highest ratings for the year and bigger than the AFL and NRL grand finals.

This would be a different challenge as Denmark started strongly with a high press and star striker Pernille Harder testing Mackenzie Arnold in goal on several occasions before we settled and began to probe the Danish defence. The match became a battle of tactics as we tried long diagonal passes to break through the tight formation while fending off Denmark's pressure at the other end of the ground.

It took a moment of brilliance to break open the encounter when, in the twenty-eighth minute, Caitlin Foord collected an errant Danish pass in the backline and made a quick pass to Mary Fowler. Mary turned, beat two opponents and looked up to see that Caitlin had kept running along the left wing. She made an inch-perfect long ball in behind the defenders which Caitlin picked up, still at top pace as she ran into the box. The keeper advanced but Caitlin, perfectly balanced, struck with her left foot, low and into the net.

The crowd erupted with a noise you could hardly imagine. Caitlin, who in a pre-match interview had challenged fans 'to be louder', played up to the scene by placing a hand to her ear before leaping, fist-pumping into the air. The crowd noise grew louder in response.

We went into the break 1–0 up but felt, like the match against Canada, that Denmark would be dangerous in the second half. Sure enough, the Danes came out fighting, with Pernille Harder the main threat, but our defence held against a rush of set-pieces.

I'd had a quiet first half but felt that my fitness would be important as the match wore on, both to thwart Denmark's capacity to launch counter-attacks and also to hopefully provide opportunities for our forwards to add a second goal. FIFA was monitoring our performances and after the match would reveal that I was covering almost 11 kilometres in every game.

We came close in the sixty-third minute when I found Caitlin on the left wing with a long ball from halfway, but even though the move broke down, it seemed just a matter of time before we scored again.

And so we did. Just seven minutes later Mary Fowler was involved in the play again as she made another lovely through ball to Kyra Cooney-Cross who played it back to Mary in the box. With a sea of Danish legs in front of her, Mary chose to pass to Emily van Egmond who, in turn, laid it off to Hayley Raso whose eyes lit up as she lashed it into the net.

As if the night could not get better, Hayley was substituted soon afterwards and Sam Kerr came onto the ground, showing no sign of the injury that had threatened to cruel her World Cup. Within minutes she showed the nous and speed that makes her such a threat, getting away from the Danish defence and shooting just over the bar.

The final whistle brought delirium inside the stadium. We had come back from the brink of embarrassment and now had a date with destiny, a quarter-final against France that could take us to a place no Australian football team had ever reached—the semi-finals of a World Cup.

Clara had been forced to return to Sweden by the time we met Denmark because she had to start pre-season training. We were chatting online one evening, two days before the match against France, when she kept being interrupted by repeated calls from an unknown number. She ignored it at first and then decided to answer. It was the police. Someone had found her father, unresponsive, in his home on Gotland Island. Peter Markstedt died soon afterwards.

It's impossible to describe how you feel in a moment like that. I had only met Peter a few times but it was enough to feel his death deeply. He had been to a few of our club matches in Sweden and told me how much he enjoyed watching me play.

I couldn't be with Clara, as much as I wanted to be. It was one of those awful occasions when your personal life clashes with your responsibilities as an athlete and a member of a team. She was very stoic and insisted that her father would have wanted me to play—and play well. That was my promise to him.

I couldn't reveal publicly what had happened—it was a private matter—but I wrote this on Instagram in an attempt to convey my feelings:

> My beautiful fiancée. Thank you for travelling to Australia to support me this World Cup. It's been so special to have you in the stands and for you to be able to spend so much time with our family & friends. We will miss you but we will see you soon . . . but not too soon 😌 i love you.

I told my team-mates in the change rooms the night of the quarter-final. I didn't say much, just that it had happened and how sad it was, but I turned around at some point and Kyra Cooney-Cross and Charli Grant had both taped on black armbands. I didn't ask them to do it; they just wanted to show me some support. Within a few minutes the rest of the team had done the same.

It was very touching, especially on the night of the most important match of our lives, and says so much about what being in the Matildas means to all of us.

The French had hammered Morocco 4–0 in their round of sixteen match and their confidence was riding high as they began the match well. You could feel the Brisbane crowd's nervousness as the French threatened to score on several occasions.

But, just like the match against Denmark, we settled and, as the daylight faded, we found our stride. We had the best chance of the half when Hayley Raso made a run down the right side and crossed to the top post where Emily van Egmond beat the keeper to the ball and tapped it back to Mary Fowler. A goal seemed inevitable until a French defender thrust out her leg to deny Mary's shot.

Sam Kerr had again started on the bench but this time Tony brought her on early in the second half as the match opened up. Now fully recovered, Sam was starting to make her presence felt as she found Hayley Raso, whose full-blooded strike forced a great save from the French keeper.

The keeper saved another Mary Fowler rocket but the match remained locked at 0–0. As we headed into extra time, things became tetchy with some late tackles and shirt pulling.

I was in a mood to get stuck in. It was a combination of things in the moment of the do-or-die match, including the death of Peter Markstedt, playing in front of my family and the joy of returning to the game I loved.

It all coalesced in those final few minutes as I charged down everything to either give us a chance to score or to stop France from scoring. Whatever it took. I copped a yellow card for a challenge on defender Sakina Karchaoui and put a slide tackle on their midfielder Grace Geyoro when things looked dangerous. I even had angry words with their captain Wendie Renard, who towered over the top of me. I can't even remember what was said between us, but there is video of me laughing so I was clearly in a mood for confrontation.

It's funny, but Dad had been warning me a couple of nights before about being too aggressive on the field. 'If you knock someone down then pick them up,' he insisted. I knew he was right, but I was having a hard time keeping my emotions in check, and I was in no mood to help any opposition player back on their feet.

We seemed beaten late in the game when the French got a lucky corner after the ball seemed to have been taken across the goal-line. From the corner kick, Alanna Kennedy unfortunately headed in an own goal, until the referee ruled that she had been fouled by Renard. We all sighed with relief.

As it became more likely that we were headed to penalties, I remember looking at the other girls. We were all thinking the same thing: that we were going to beat our penalty hoodoo and win this game no matter what. There was something about the night and the occasion that convinced me that destiny was on our side. Peter was looking down on me, and the Matildas.

And so it was. The final whistle went and we gathered for the penalty shootout, the eleven players who had been on the ground standing, locked arm in arm at halfway while the French sat in a group.

The drama of the next few minutes is worth reliving.

Left-back Selma Bacha went first for France as Mackenzie Arnold prowled around the goal-line then moved to the right and saved the penalty. The stadium erupted as Bacha wandered disconsolately back to her team-mates: 0–0.

Caitlin Foord was next. Could she score and give the Matildas the early advantage? Yes, she could as she slammed it low and left: 0–1 Australia!

French forward Kadidiatou Diani walked out, ignoring the giant screens at either end of the ground which showed a replay of Caitlin's goal, then rolling her penalty calmly to the bottom right corner: 1–1.

Steph Catley had already scored two great penalties in the tournament. Would she go to the same side? Yes, but she wasn't wide or hard enough as the French keeper, Solene Durand, who'd come on as a substitute, guessed correctly and made a comfortable save. The crowd groaned. Back on level terms again: 1–1.

Renard frowned in concentration as she took France's next kick, luring Macca to the right with her body angle before swivelling as she kicked and striking it left to score: France 2–1.

Sam Kerr, the weight of expectation on her shoulders, squeezed it past Durand, who again read it correctly but just failed to get a glove on the ball: 2–2.

Eugenie Le Sommer, France's leading all-time scorer, calmly fired it into the bottom right-hand corner: France 3–2.

Mary Fowler, brimming with confidence, hammered the ball low and left into the net, giving the keeper no chance: 3–3.

Eve Perisset went left but so did Mackenzie who tipped the ball into the side post and kept it out: 3–3.

Suddenly Australia was one kick away from a semi-final berth as Macca herself walked to the spot. If she converted, the team would make history. Watching from halfway I knew how she would be feeling, heart pumping wildly as she tried to settle her nerves and execute something she'd done countless times in training. She struck it beautifully to the right but it was slightly wide, hit the upright and bounced away: 3–3.

The crowd, which was now on its collective feet, groaned again. We were going to extra penalties which meant that one miss and we were history.

Grace Geyoro stuttered as she ran in, as if to unsettle Mackenzie who could not prevent the goal: France 4–3.

It was my turn. I would tell people later that in the excitement I didn't even realise that we were out if I missed. I had erased the Brazil regrets from my mind and just concentrated on what I had been doing in training. I had already decided to go to the left and hit it hard, hopefully giving the keeper little chance.

I waited for the whistle and struck the ball as hard as possible, then watched in horror as the keeper moved the same way. She got her hands into the path of the ball but it burst through them and into the net. (It was measured at 106.33 kilometres per hour, the third hardest goal of the tournament.) 4–4.

As I ran back towards my team-mates I kissed a wristband on my left forearm. It had Peter Markstedt written on it, then rocked my arms as in a cradle. The goal was for Peter and Harper.

Sakina Karchaoui belted her kick high and right, past Mackenzie before it hit the bottom of the crossbar and into the net: France 5–4.

Tameka Yallop's face was set in stone as she paused at the top of her run-up before almost trotting in and rolling the ball into the bottom right-hand corner: 5–5.

Maelle Lakrar did not hesitate and rocketed her shot into the top right-hand corner: France 6–5.

Ellie Carpenter curled the ball left and in off the woodwork: 6–6.

Midfielder Kenza Dali was next for France. She looked nervous and Macca could see it, guessed correctly and dived to her left, making a great save. We leaped for joy as Kenza sunk to her knees but the lineswoman ruled that Macca had moved too early and the kick should be retaken. Would the Frenchwoman go the same way or change her tactic? Of course not; Macca feinted one way and then back the same way as the previous penalty, made the same save. This time Kenza put her hands to her head in disappointment as now the crowd leaped with joy: 6–6.

The future was riding on Clare Hunt's young shoulders as she walked to the spot. She had been in the team for just a few months and yet it was her responsibility to see us through to the semi-final. She chose to go down the middle, only to have Solene Durand, who had gone to her right, fling one hand back and effect the save. Heartbreak for Clare and Australia: 6–6.

Vicki Becho, who had been subbed late in the game, went left as Macca went right, but the ball was a fraction wide and hit the upright. Australia, once again, had a kick for glory.

Tony appealed for calm from the sideline as Cortnee Vine stepped forward to be the heroine. She said later that she hadn't expected to have to take a kick, so had lost count of the number taken before realising that it was her turn.

In fact, she couldn't remember ever having to take one in a match situation.

There were no nerves visible as she stood frowning at the ball, visualising what she had done so many times in training: 'Macca had made it easy for me by saving those penalties,' she would say. 'All I had to do was put it away'. And that's what she did, taking only three or four steps before jamming the ball with authority into the net, then turning and sprinting back towards us.

'Cue the party,' yelled the television commentator above the roar of the Brisbane crowd as we leaped on each other and screamed with delight. It was the longest penalty shootout in World Cup history—ten shots by each nation—and we had triumphed as I knew we would:

Never in doubt 👊

I wrote that later on Instagram. I meant it.

The crowd applauded us for what seemed like hours as we lapped up our achievement. I ran across to my family and we hugged and kissed before I grabbed Harper and took her onto the ground. The crowd cheered louder as we waved. She didn't seem fazed by the noise.

Oh, I forgot to mention, I was turning thirty-one the next day; what a birthday present!

CHAPTER TWENTY-SIX

Milestones and Misery

My birthday was quiet. I couldn't really let my hair down. Not only was our upcoming game against England a semi-final but it was also my hundredth game for the Matildas. Birthdays and milestones, crowds of 75,000-plus amid a fantastic experience I could never really have dreamed could happen.

The television and streaming figures for the quarter-final against France were mind-boggling—an average audience of 4.17 million—the biggest event of the year and not even counting the thousands who watched at clubs, pubs, sporting venues and dozens of live site broadcasts around Australia.

We had come so far from that cold spring day in Sydney in 2015 when the girls and I stood in the park outside the Football Federation Australia office, waiting to see if we were going to get a decent wage rise only to be told that we didn't deserve one because we weren't worth it commercially.

Now everyone wanted a part of our success. It wasn't a matter of *them* or *they* but *we* and *us*. You could see and hear it at the live sites in our cities and towns as fans gathered to watch our games. There were wigs and hats and drums and flags and banners, all green and gold of course. The crowds sang traditional football songs—'Ole, Ole, Ole'—and chanted for 'our Tillies'.

As news of our win was broadcast by other TV stations there was vision of happy crowds, interviewed as they celebrated long into the night. 'We did it, we did it!' shouted two middle-aged men who probably had never been to a Matildas game. 'Best night of my life. Best night of my fucking life,' cried a twenty-something woman trying to find her Matildas jersey under her jacket to show her fandom.

Australia was suddenly a football-loving nation, not because the Socceroos had played well but because the Matildas—the women's team—were a real contender to go all the way and win the World Cup.

But we were not the only team playing with expectation. The Lionesses were playing for history as much as we were, with the burden of England football's long wait for international glory. No team had made a World Cup final since their victory in 1966. And now the women's team had a chance to end the nightmare—'football's coming home', as their anthem says.

Their form leading up to the tournament had been impressive, winning Euro 22 the previous July by beating

Germany 2–1 in a nail-biting final, a replay of the 1966 men's World Cup final played at Wembley Stadium.

In the World Cup to this point they had been steady rather than spectacular, winning their three pool matches against Haiti (1–0), Denmark (1–0) and China (6–1) before sneaking past Nigeria 4–2 on penalties after the match finished 0–0 in the round of sixteen, and then coming from behind to beat Colombia 2–1 in the quarter-final.

The match began with a bang as both sides came close to scoring from long balls played in behind the defences, first the Matildas when I sent a long ball over the top of the English defenders from behind the halfway line and found Sam Kerr whose first-time strike was thwarted by English goalkeeper Mary Earps, and then England a few minutes later when Georgia Stanway forced a great save from Mackenzie Arnold after a sensational long ball by Alex Greenwood.

The chances went back and forth as the nerves disappeared and it was clear that, unlike our match against France, there would be goals at some point, and plenty of them. Spaces were opening up as England began to dominate and in the twenty-ninth minute Ella Toone smashed in a stinging shot after the ball had been kept in play at the back line by Lauren Hemp.

It was a wake-up call for us, and getting to half-time at 1–0 down was a relief. We were still in the game but needed to score next if we were going to get past the Lionesses and into the final.

The answer came through Sam Kerr, of course. In the sixty-third minute I slipped the ball to her near the halfway line and she sprinted forward towards goal. The two English defenders, Millie Bright and Jess Carter, who happened to be Sam's Chelsea clubmates, kept backing away which only encouraged Sam as she approached the top of the box and unleashed a powerhouse shot that flew over and past the goalkeeper and into the roof of the net.

It was 1–1 and Stadium Australia found its voice. I can only imagine the mini eruptions at the live sites across the country. We were back level and with momentum, but it was England who steadied and just ten minutes later had restored their lead when Lauren Hemp, who had looked dangerous all game, won a goalmouth tussle with Ellie Carpenter and slotted the ball past Mackenzie.

We didn't give up as Sam had a couple more chances, including a rebound shot from a few metres that just went over the bar as she clapped her hands to her mouth in disappointment.

Then England drove the final nail into our coffin when, with just five minutes left on the clock, Lauren Hemp got the ball midfield, took it forward and put a ball through for Alessia Russo who hit it first time past a diving Mackenzie.

I was interviewed at the side of the ground while the English celebrations went on behind me. I was shattered like the other girls, particularly as it was my hundredth game for the Matildas, but I was circumspect too.

'I guess that's football,' I said simply. 'Sometimes you win and sometimes you lose. It's just a crappy time to lose, I guess. I thought we created lots of chances and kept possession well in patches and we put a lot of pressure on them. We couldn't get the ball in the back of the net and they did.'

There was little consolation the next day when the television figures were released, the highest-rating program in the history of Australian television—a peak audience of 11.15 million people with an average during the match of 7.13 million. The only other event that came close was the night in 2000 when another proud Australian woman, Cathy Freeman, won Olympic gold in the 400 metres.

—

I'd rather not dwell on the bronze medal match against Sweden three nights later. The stands at the Brisbane Stadium were packed with almost 50,000 fans and the television audience, although not quite as large as the semi-final match, still numbered just under three million.

The signs were there early in the game that we were going to struggle when Swedish striker Stina Blackstenius fired a low drive across the goal which was gloved away by Mackenzie Arnold. Even though Hayley Raso came close to scoring soon afterwards, it was Sweden who held sway through the first half.

Disaster struck in the twenty-sixth minute when Sweden mounted yet another attack and the ball was slipped through to Blackstenius who ran into the box under pressure from Clare Hunt. Blackstenius passed back to a team-mate, but as she did so she went down. The VAR replay showed that she had been tripped by Clare Hunt and a penalty was given. Forward Fridolina Rolfo calmly put away the penalty to give Sweden a 1–0 lead.

I could feel that the team was struggling. It wasn't that we lacked the desire to win but as the exhilaration of the French victory began to deflate there was an exhaustion, physically and mentally.

I was as frustrated as anyone, so tired from the French drama and English disappointment that I didn't train the day before just to have a rest and freshen up. During the game I forced myself to run and tackle hard, which earned me a warning and a yellow card. In the last few minutes of the half I was brought down by the Swedish captain Kosovare Asllani and given a free kick. When she continued to stand over me my emotions got the better of me. I struggled to my feet and shoved her to let her know that she was in the wrong. Steph Catley and Clare Polkinghorne came rushing in to stop me from boiling over. The photos later showed the anger in my eyes.

Half-time couldn't come quickly enough. We needed to regather ourselves if we stood a chance of finding an equaliser and finishing the tournament on a high.

There were signs of hope early in the second half but we simply weren't as fluid as we had been in previous matches. I came off, as planned, and was replaced by Cortnee Vine as Tony tried to ring changes that might produce the goal we needed, but it was Sweden who struck.

Just past the hour mark Blackstenius was again in the action, squaring the ball to Asllani who rifled a shot from the edge of the area into the top right-hand corner as Mackenzie dived in vain.

Sweden 2–0.

There seemed no way back a few minutes later when Sam Kerr went down and needed treatment. Clare Polkinghorne hammered a volley only for it to be saved, Clare Hunt had a go as did Mary Fowler, Kyra Cooney-Cross and Emily van Egmond. But it was all to no avail as the final whistle went. Our dream was over.

Tony summed up our feelings at the post-match press conference.

'It's a difficult moment to find the right words right now. We're hurt, we wanted to bring a medal for this team, these fans and this nation. It's now a second tournament that we played for a medal and missed out. Maybe we won something bigger than a medal though. It's difficult now but when we distance ourselves and look forward. I love working with these players and this team. I don't see this tournament as an end to a journey but a beginning. I am excited by next year's Olympics in Paris.'

Statistics don't always tell you the full story but FIFA's measurements released in the weeks after Spain beat England 1–0 to raise the trophy show where my efforts lay. I covered almost 75 kilometres in seven matches, but the most significant number was the fifty-nine tackles I made—fifteen more than any other player in the tournament.

When I returned to Sweden a few months later I was surprised to be told that I was on a shortlist for Swedish Citizen of the Year because my performances had helped promote the Hassleholm region. It reminded me again how much positive influence sport can have on everyday life.

CHAPTER TWENTY-SEVEN
The Cycle of Life

Major events can often mark the end of a journey and the beginning of a new experience. I felt that moment as the hype and joy of the World Cup began to wear off and Clara and I looked ahead to the arrival of our new baby.

We could have stayed in Sweden and played another season or two with Vittsjo but I felt that I still had unexplored experiences, in particular the Women's Super League in England where a number of my Matildas team-mates had gone in recent seasons, most notably Sam Kerr who was playing at Chelsea.

Matildas goalkeeper Mackenzie Arnold had been at West Ham since 2020 and had nothing but nice things to say about the club. I had also come to know Icelandic player Dagny Brynjarsdottir, who'd had a baby and was pregnant with her second. West Ham had been very supportive and had even made a documentary detailing her journey as a player and mother, and the challenges and barriers faced by female athletes when starting a family.

It was a live issue for us because Clara was now pregnant. We had both wanted to have a child together and decided to use the three spare embryos I had stored at the Norway clinic. There were various reasons for this, partly due to the timing of everything around the World Cup, but also because Clara has polycystic ovary syndrome, which can affect fertility. It seemed a sensible option to try the stored embryos, and if one of them didn't take then we would try again after the World Cup.

As had happened for me, the first embryo took and Clara discovered she was pregnant a few days after we had returned to Sweden to attend her father's funeral. I remember waking up one morning, looking over at Clara. Her boobs were massive and I said: 'I think we should try a pregnancy test.'

Sure enough, there was a faint positive line and when we retested a day or so later the line was clear. If all went well, the baby was due a few weeks before the Olympic Games in Paris. Life is forever complicated, but in a wonderful way.

The Hammers seemed to be the perfect club for me, not only because of their family-friendly attitude but because they were in the middle of the pack performance-wise, I was guaranteed game time and my experience could be of value. Winning titles and trophies is amazing but it's not the be-all and end-all of team sport; having influence and helping people improve gives me just as much satisfaction as raising silverware.

I asked Macca, who was being made captain, to put in a good word for me and by January 2024 I had signed a three-and-a-half-year contract. It came just at the right time: Clara was pregnant and decided that she wanted to retire from football to concentrate on her business and family life. I didn't feel that I was finished yet as a footballer, but we both felt that stability—financially and physically—was now an important aspect of our lives.

The hardest thing was choosing a number. Numbers ten and nineteen were already taken so Clara and I thought about it for a while. For some reason, the number twenty-two kept coming up in our lives—the date of Clara's dad's funeral (22 September) and the likely birthdate of the baby (22 June), so that's what I chose.

The cultural difference between the English and Australian domestic competitions is massive.

The women's game is growing rapidly in the UK where fans live and breathe club football, not just international games. People are interested in the women's game as well as the men's.

The Matildas captured the Australian public's attention but in Australia club games are still played in front of a few thousand people. The highest attendance was in October 2023, just after the World Cup, when 11,471 watched a match in Sydney. Compare that to a fixture in London in December that year when more than 59,000 fans filled the Emirates Stadium to watch Arsenal beat Chelsea. In England, people know me when I go into restaurants and walk down the street.

I immediately felt at home at West Ham. Even though I was coming into the club halfway through the season, I could sense there was respect for what I could bring to the team and a lot of support for Clara and Harper off the ground.

I felt an enjoyment of being part of something new without the expectation that came with the Matildas' search for international triumph. It took me back in some ways to my junior days when I was on the field to have fun and do my best.

Then came the injury.

I had been nursing a niggling calf injury for a few weeks when we lined up to play against Chelsea. It was a big game in front of a decent crowd and I desperately wanted to play with the calf strapped. I was naturally wary of it as we played, unconsciously protecting it. Things were fine and I was playing well until I went to intercept a ball and got pulled back by an opposition player.

I went over on my right ankle and I felt a kind of pop, so loud it sounded like my boot had come off. I knew straight away that it was bad, and as soon as I stood up the pain went through me like someone had shot me. I hobbled off the ground and lay there while the physios tinkered around my leg, typically not saying much as if they don't really want to tell you the truth.

I asked if it was my syndesmosis because it felt so similar to the left ankle injury I'd got at Brisbane. The scans confirmed the worst. I needed surgery, to basically tie my ankle bones together, and at least three months rehab, which meant that unless everything went perfectly, I wasn't going to the Olympics.

Tony was understanding but he must have been spewing, given that Sam Kerr had been ruled out with an ACL injury. He was very supportive though and told me not to worry: 'If the ankle is right then I'm taking you.'

—

Clara was getting quite big by May and she wanted to be home in Sweden for the later stages of the pregnancy. It meant we had to make the journey from London sooner than we had planned and I'd have to finish my rehab by myself, perhaps back at Vittsjo if they'd have me.

I had left the club on good terms and they were happy to help out. The assistant coach Thomas Martensson was still at the club and arranged a physio and for young players to come and help me out at sessions. It really made a difference because it's no fun training on your own.

In the meantime Clara was getting ever bigger and at one point there were concerns that she might have pre-eclampsia. Thankfully the fears died away as we tried to finalise a name for what we now knew would be a little boy.

Choosing Harper's name was easy because I didn't have to please anyone else, but this was more complex. We wanted a name that might not be a Swedish name but could be pronounced easily by Swedish people. We shied away from popular names and had a few options, including Koby, Hudson and Aston.

After umming and aahing for a while, we both decided one night that we liked the sound of Koby and besides, Harper and Koby sound cute together. He also has two middle names—Peter, after Clara's late father and my dad, and David, after my stepdad who has been Mum's partner for twenty-five years and an important part of my life.

It was a Friday when things started to happen. We had been expecting him for days and nothing was moving despite confident predictions that showed he was in the birth canal and ready to pop out.

Mum and David were over from Australia and we'd gone to the beach for the day. I'd even relaxed and was having a gin and tonic. When Mum suggested that tonight might be the night, I dismissed the idea.

Around midnight Clara rolled over and woke me. 'Babe, my waters have broken.' I asked if she was sure and maybe she should go back to sleep, but she insisted: 'The bed's soaking wet.'

I was suddenly awake and rushed around trying to clean up the house in the middle of the night to make things nice while she settled on the couch as the contractions started.

We tried to distract ourselves and watched a series on TV but by 9 am we decided it was time to go into the hospital so she could get checked. Clara settled into the room but by 4 pm she had still only dilated three centimetres and she was exhausted from the contractions. So was I.

Clara had made the decision not to use any drugs, but a couple of hours later the midwife came in, noticed how tired she looked and asked if she would accept a morphine shot. She relented reluctantly. By 10 pm she was still only seven centimetres and I suggested she consider an epidural.

'The last thing you want is an emergency caesarean because you're exhausted and he's exhausted.'

'But I feel so guilty. I said I didn't want drugs.'

'It's fine, babe. It's fine; it's just where you're at.'

She got the epidural and we both fell asleep for a couple of hours. It was about seven o'clock the next morning before she started pushing and it would take another three hours before Koby finally arrived. It had been more than thirty-four hours since Clara had woken me.

I helped to get him out but it was clear that something was wrong. He wasn't making a sound and he was deathly white. They cut the umbilical cord and took him away to ICU. I followed, covered in blood and wondering what was happening.

The nurses were speaking in Swedish so I couldn't really understand what was going on. Eventually they told me that he hadn't taken a breath, perhaps from the shock of his entry into the world. He would have to go on a breathing tube or he 'might be really angry at the world and just scream it out'. I waited, nervously, not knowing what to do and wondering if Clara was okay upstairs. Luckily, Koby must have been angry because he screamed his lungs out, and everything was okay.

The next day I announced his arrival on Instagram alongside a photo of Harper hugging her baby brother.

> Our sweet baby boy arrived at 10.36 am. Big sister is absolutely in love and our hearts are full.

For Clara, the emotions were even stronger, as she wrote:

> An emotional roller coaster saying goodbye to my dad, finding out we're pregnant just days later, ending my football career, moving countries and experiencing the beauty and struggles with pregnancy. Now he is here and I couldn't be happier or more grateful for this journey and for my beautiful family. Thank you @katrinagorry10 for being my rock through it all, for being my role model as a mum, for always making me laugh, for supporting me through these nine months, 34 hours of labor to then delivering our beautiful son into this world. I love you more than words can describe ♡

CHAPTER TWENTY-EIGHT
Nightmare in Marseille

The Matildas had ploughed their way through the second round of Olympic qualifications in October 2023, beating Iran 2–0, the Philippines 8–0 and Chinese Taipei 3–0 in a round-robin event played in Perth, our performances good enough to finish on top of the table and earning a playoff against Uzbekistan while Japan and North Korea would fight for the other available place.

Our playoff game was over two legs, the first played in Tashkent on 24 February, where we initially struggled but scored three late goals to take an almost unassailable lead going into the return match in Melbourne four nights later in front of a crowd of 54,120.

The match was a one-sided affair and a personal triumph for my roomie Michelle Heyman who had returned to the team after a five-year absence. She had scored four goals before being subbed off at half-time—as was I—on our way to a 10–0 win.

It's done, shouted the specially printed team banners erected on the ground afterwards as we celebrated what was more of a relief than anything else, given there were thirty-one teams who had entered for the two spots from the Asia region.

England, by comparison, had missed out despite its fantastic performances in 2023, unable to win one of the semi-finals of the UEFA Nations League tournament. Instead, Spain, France and Germany won their way through to Paris.

It was late March before the draw was made for the Olympic tournament—three groups of four teams with the top two in each group plus the two best third-place teams going through to the knockout stages.

The groups were drawn by taking a team each from four FIFA-ranked 'pots'. The highest-ranked teams—Spain, France and the USA—were in pot 1; Germany, Japan and Canada in pot 2; Brazil, ourselves and Colombia in pot 3; and New Zealand, Nigeria and Zambia in pot 4.

Whoever we drew, it meant that we had to beat two teams ranked above us by FIFA, or beat the third, lower team by a score large enough to ensure we finished the best-placed third team. The balls were drawn and the task was set. Our first round opponents would be the USA, Germany and Zambia.

As Tony noted afterwards, it didn't matter who we drew; it was going to be tough just to get out of the group stage. We would play Germany first followed by Zambia and then the USA, who had dominated women's football at the Olympics with four gold medals.

There was something different about the team vibe from the moment we arrived at our training camp in Marbella, Spain. It's hard to be specific, but we didn't feel as connected as we had before and during the World Cup.

The preparation hadn't been as co-ordinated and half-a-dozen players, myself, Steph Catley, Kaitlyn Torpey and Teagan Micah among them, were getting over injuries while others had been training on home programs, so match fitness had become an issue. And we undoubtedly felt the loss of Sam Kerr for the second big tournament in a row.

The camp was also very different in the sense that for the first week we could all have our partners with us. I'm not suggesting that this impacted on our performance in a negative way, but we spent less time together between training sessions. And once the tournament started we all had rooms to ourselves. Times had changed.

It is inevitable in those circumstances that pockets of people start forming, each with their own opinions and grievances about the way things are being handled. I felt it, I saw it and I heard it and one of my regrets is that I didn't stand up and say something so that we all felt more connected.

I was happy personally. My ankle injury had healed well and I had no doubts that it would hold up, although my match fitness was down, which meant I had to accept that I would have to have a measured return to game time. I didn't want to blow out in the first game; it was better to play sixty minutes or so and then bring on a fresh player like Clare Wheeler.

There are four scenarios for the first match in a tournament. You can win, you can draw, you can lose—and you can lose badly.

We believed we could beat Germany, even though we hadn't done so in almost two decades, and we expected to at least draw the match. Losing by a goal, say 1–0 or 2–1, would have been disappointing but manageable in terms of getting through the group stage, but a two or three goal deficit would be disastrous, given the task ahead against the USA in particular.

It was clear from the first few minutes of the match that Germany was ready to perform and we were going to struggle in the stifling heat of Marseille.

Their attack looked ominous and was led by winger Jule Brand who launched several early solo runs, and almost opened the scoring in the tenth minute. Luckily her shot sailed over the bar, while we struggled to create chances against a solid German defence, not helped by some poor passing.

I don't think we were supporting each other enough to break the German team down. We were moving the ball too slowly and turning it over in dangerous areas. To compound our problems, Steph Catley went down injured after a head clash and, although she recovered, our rhythm and cohesiveness seemed off. In hindsight, I can see now that it was that nagging feeling I'd had in camp about the team vibe that seemed missing.

A German goal seemed inevitable and eventually came in the twenty-fourth minute from a corner kick which floated to the back post where their centre back Marina Hegering rose, unchallenged, to head the ball home. Mary Fowler almost equalised from the restart but her shot was blocked by a desperate lunge and we played out the rest of the half trying to keep our deficit to just one goal.

We regrouped at half-time, confident we could haul back the goal if we could make the most of our chances and dampen the Germans' counter-attacks.

For a while things looked more promising, with Mary again into the action after a nice run down the left wing by Steph, but we were struggling against Jule Brand who unleashed two cracking shots, one just wide and the other just over the crossbar.

I came off in the fiftieth minute as agreed with Tony before the game to protect my ankle. It was frustrating because I'd played well and felt comfortable in the midfield. Even though we were being pounded, it felt that we were still in the game at this stage and an equaliser was possible. But it was not to be.

The killer blow came in the sixty-fourth minute when forward Lea Schuller leaped the highest and nodded in a corner kick. For a brief moment on the restart it looked as though substitute Sharn Freier, fed by a lovely through ball from Steph, might answer quickly but the move broke down and four minutes later Jule Brand added a third goal when she neatly trapped a low cross at the far post.

Tony made another series of changes with twenty minutes left, bringing on Michelle Heyman, Emily van Egmond and Kaitlyn Torpey. It seemed to spur the players on as Clare Hunt, Ellie Carpenter and Kyra Cooney-Cross all came close but the match petered out and the final whistle confirmed our worst fears.

It was no good trying to pretend that all was well, and Tony ended up issuing an apology to our fans and promising a better performance against Zambia. The match was just three days away, which is a short turnaround given the hot weather and the fact that we had to travel 200 kilometres up the coast to the city of Nice where Zambia were already based.

We spent the time trying to regroup and ignoring the surge of angry social media comments from back in Australia where critics, including some from the media who should have known better, were calling for Tony's head and accusing us of being pampered.

Australia sees itself as a proud sporting nation and yet there seems to be little tolerance for what is perceived to be 'failure' rather than the reality and pressures of playing sport at an elite level. It brought back memories of the criticism we faced for daring to stand up for ourselves and demand fair pay and conditions.

I tried to ignore the comments but the negativity inevitably affects team morale, so all the critics achieved was to make things harder for us.

A couple of hours before our match in the city of Saint-Etienne, 340 kilometres north of Marseille, New Zealand was playing Canada. The Kiwis had scored first against the defending Olympic champions before the Canadians struck back and then scored a winner late in the game.

But there was a scandal brewing. A couple of days before the game, New Zealand players had noticed a drone flying above them during training sessions. They complained to police who followed the drone to its operator—a member of the Canadian coaching team.

It turned out that the Canadian women's and men's teams had been using drones to spy on competitors for several years. The team apologised and several staff were sent home, but New Zealand protested and Canada was docked the three points for the win as well as another three points, meaning they were on −6 after one round. The team appealed but it was dismissed.

The upshot was that it gave us some hope despite our dismal performance against Germany, but we still needed a big win against the Zambians. What we got was unexpected, infuriating and exciting, one of the craziest matches in Olympic history.

Zambia qualified for the Games by reaching the semi-finals of the Women's Africa Cup of Nations—a significant milestone because it was the first time an African landlocked nation of either sex had qualified. Their Olympic campaign had begun the same way as ours, a 3–0 loss, although it was a decent effort against the USA.

Despite its FIFA ranking of just sixty-four, the team boasted two of the most highly paid forwards in the game. Racheal Kundananji had just signed a US$788,000 transfer with American club Bay FC, and team-mate Barbra Banda had signed a US$740,000 transfer fee to Orlando Pride.

We knew they were both dangerous and we talked a lot about the speed and skill of the Zambian forwards. We needed to score goals but we needed to be mindful of their threat in transition and off the break. What we didn't expect was to face them on a day when everything they touched turned to gold, or should I say goal.

It began in the first minute of the game when Banda got onto a pass, turned the defence inside out and unleashed a strike that flew over Mackenzie Arnold's outstretched hands into the net.

We were stunned—a nightmare upon a nightmare—but things seemed back on track just six minutes later when Alanna Kennedy timed her run into the box to convert Steph Catley's free kick with an easy header: 1–1.

Could we settle and exert some sustained pressure on the Copper Queens, as they call themselves. The answer was no, as Kundananji showed her star quality by stealing the ball midfield, driving through our defence and slotting the ball home across the face of goal.

We were clearly in trouble and it only got worse as Banda scored again in the thirty-third minute, smashing it home after Mackenzie had palmed away a free kick: 1–3 behind.

To our credit we struck back a minute or so later after winning a corner kick. Kyra Cooney-Cross found Hayley Raso at the back post and she headed home to bring us back to 2–3.

With ten minutes left in the first half there had already been five goals scored as we struggled to keep pace. It wasn't over yet as Banda stepped up again, this time when an attempted clear by Emily van Egmond cannoned off her foot and into the goal: 2–4 at half-time.

The mood inside our change rooms at half-time was surprisingly positive despite our dire situation. It wasn't as if we weren't creating chances. I'd had three myself, including a rare header, so we felt that we were still in the game. It was a matter of taking each chance as it came and tightening up on Banda and Kundananji.

The second half began in the worst possible way when Banda played a perfect pass to Kundananji who didn't break stride as she headed home for Zambia's fifth, and a three-goal lead.

Tony responded by making a triple change, bringing on Kaitlyn Torpey, Clare Wheeler and Michelle Heyman who immediately got into the action when she back-heeled the ball in the goalmouth only for a Zambian defender to cut it off on the line and then turn it into her own net: 3–5.

We could hope again as we piled on the pressure. A fourth goal was disallowed before a bit of luck came our way when a Steph Catley shot from twenty metres went through the Zambian keeper's hands: 4–5.

We threw caution to the wind as we searched for an equaliser. It came with barely ten minutes left when Caitlin Foord was fouled in the box and Steph stepped up and made no mistake. We were back on terms at 5–5 with time to find a winner in this most ridiculous of games.

There were chances at both ends in the dying minutes, first for Kundananji and then Michelle but the scores were still tied with one minute left. Kyra won the ball in defence and played it to Steph in the centre of the ground. She played a delicate pass to Michelle who managed to beat the offside trap and calmly slide the ball past the advancing keeper into the right-hand netting for a sixth, and winning goal.

Michelle raced off with one arm raised in the air in triumph. Somehow, from the depths of despair, our fighting spirit as a team had shone through and saved our Olympic campaign, at least for the moment. I had tears in my eyes watching from the bench. It was such a proud moment for my friend.

Tony did not mince his words after the game: 'This is not the time to dwell on how we conceded five goals because obviously that was shit. Right now we are focusing on the spirit and energy we used to get this done and turn the game around.'

Despite the win, our chances of progressing depended mostly on the results of other games. In our own group, the USA had thrashed Germany 4–1 later the same night which opened up possibilities if we could beat the Americans or if Zambia could beat Germany, which seemed possible but unlikely.

Our other hope was that the stricken Canadians would struggle against France, giving us another route to the knockouts by being the best third-placed team. Instead, Canada repeated their effort against New Zealand and came back from a goal behind to beat the host nation 2–1 which, remarkably, kept them in the race given that their goal difference was positive.

But we couldn't worry too much about possibilities. What was clear was that a win over the USA or at least a draw would almost certainly mean we would go through and keep alive our hopes to finally win a medal at a major tournament.

The thing that bothered me most was that we are good at coming together when we win in tight circumstances, but what we really need to do better is to be able to close ranks and come together as a team when we lose.

Hindsight is a wonderful thing but foresight is better, they say, and our match against the USA at Marseille on 31 July is a great case in point.

We had two outcomes that would ensure we progressed to the knockout rounds—win or draw—so how do you play tactically to give yourself the best chance of one of those aims? And given that we had only beaten the USA once in thirty-four encounters, a draw seemed more likely than a victory. We had done exactly that four years before at the group stage.

Tony decided that we should play a patient game in which we mirrored their shape. We knew they liked to push their fullbacks on forward so we needed extra cover by having five players back. Even though the Americans dominated possession—with seventy-two per cent of the ball—we formed a much more cohesive defensive unit than our wayward performance against Zambia.

But there was a price to pay. As Australians we love to attack and press, using our pace up forward to get in behind the opposition defence. We're good at it. But in this more defensive formation we didn't have that opportunity because, as much as we worked defensively, when we did get the ball back we didn't have the players higher up the field to create the chances we needed to score.

Still, we achieved our aim to keep the USA forwards quiet for all but the last few minutes of regular time in the first half when an in-swinging corner kick by the USA was headed back towards the goalmouth where forward Trinity Rodman managed to toe-poke it past Mackenzie Arnold.

There was some controversy about the goal but a VAR review confirmed that all our hard work had been undone in a goalmouth scramble and we went in at half-time now requiring at least one goal to get the draw we needed.

We started the second half brightly with a more positive 4–4–2 shape and playing a more aggressive brand of football with Michelle and Emily on the ground. But chances were few and far between and the Americans were a constant threat. I came off midway through the half, frustrated because my injured ankle was fine, I was playing well and winning the ball back, and we had nothing to lose at this stage. The tournament was over for us unless we could find at least one goal.

Our hopes held until the last twelve minutes of the game when an attempted clearance from defence fell to US midfielder Korbin Albert who unleashed a powerful strike that found the top left-hand side of the net.

We were now two goals down and the task looked almost hopeless although we continued to push hard even in the ninetieth minute when Alanna Kennedy finally scored as she connected with a flick-on from Michelle Heyman. Alanna grabbed the ball from the net and rushed it back to the middle for a restart but time was against us as the Americans won 2–1.

When Canada beat Colombia 1–0 a few hours later it confirmed that we had fallen at the group hurdle and our dreams of an Olympic medal had been extinguished. I don't think I have ever felt so crushed, but there was one positive for me—it ended any thoughts of retirement I may have had. There is no way I would walk away on such a downer.

There were bound to be repercussions as public expectation had been so high and it was clear that Tony's head was on the chopping block. It's a tough school for coaches and managers. Five years is a long time for a coach of any team. If you are successful then everyone loves you, but when things go sour people want you out.

Tony did a lot for the team in terms of playing style and I can't thank him enough for the way he treated me and my family. But I recognise that maybe things had become a little complacent and we needed fresh eyes and ideas. A new coach will bring new perspective and the team has to be excited by that prospect.

CHAPTER TWENTY-NINE

New Challenges

As I write this I am getting used to a new role—captain of the West Ham United women's football team.

It is the first time in my career that I have been asked to lead. I have always seen myself as an on-field manager, and been vice-captain at Brisbane Roar, but I had not really considered formally taking the captain's role until the club asked me.

I understand why people talk about it being an honour. I couldn't stop grinning as I put on an armband with the word *Captain* for the club's pre-season promotional shoots. It adds another level to my sense of achievement.

The future is a strange thing to contemplate at the age of thirty-two. People of my age who have, shall we say, more 'normal' careers would be thinking about being in the middle of their working lives and looking at ways to advance themselves, but sportspeople of my age are starting to consider the end of a career and the beginning of a new life.

I don't want to plan too far ahead. I am committed to West Ham for the next two seasons and I definitely want to play with the Matildas in another Asia Cup in 2026, which will be in Australia and is part of the qualification for the 2027 World Cup in Brazil.

Beyond that, I'll have to wait and see how my body holds up. If it does and I'm still enjoying my football then of course I'd love to play in another World Cup before the 2028 Olympics in Los Angeles. We'll have to wait and see.

Beyond football I know two things: first, I have no desire to coach. I reckon coaches are crazy. It's tough enough handling two kids at home, let alone trying to herd twenty of them into a co-ordinated group.

It also seems to be that coaches get a rough time, with little to gain unless they achieve the ultimate and win a major trophy, and even then they will be judged on what happens afterwards. It's not always fair and I've felt particularly sorry for people like Tony Gustavsson who end up being the focus of fan and club frustration rather than the whole team—players and administrators—taking a share of the responsibility.

The other thing I know for certain is that I want to stay involved in the game that I adore. The role would probably be in the area of player management where I can be involved with younger players on a personal level. From my own experience—I've had some good managers and I've had some terrible ones—I feel that players need close-up, personal support rather than being a number in a stable. Contracts aren't just about the dollars.

The game has changed enormously since I began playing professionally. There is now money and opportunity in the women's game and clubs are taking more seriously the need to support young women, not just as sportswomen but as people. But there are still challenges, particularly how to nurture young talent and avoid people burning out and losing confidence.

I feel strongly about the lack of understanding when it comes to nutrition. I still hear people in the locker room comparing skin folds, as if having less makes you a better player. I simply don't understand why these tests are used by clubs to pressure young women into certain eating behaviours when science tells us that this is not the case.

Women are all different and we go through different menstrual cycles. How does a machine know when I'm having my period or take into account that I've had a baby?

My body hasn't changed a lot over the years although I am much stronger now than when I started. Extra muscle requires extra nourishment, not fasting and weight loss. I attain endurance by training, not because my skin fold has dropped.

Dealing with mental health is also critical, especially finding ways to help players to talk about their ups and their downs without the fear that they will be misunderstood or discarded for being difficult to manage. The misuse of social media, in particular, can add yet another level of negative pressure that can pile up on young minds.

Speaking of social media reminds me about fans. They have been an integral part of my career and the rise of women's sport in Australia. The exhilaration of seeing the stands full during the World Cup and the noise of their joy when we beat France in that quarter-final will stay with me forever.

I have been lucky enough to have had some wonderful, personal moments with supporters through my career. They seem to like me, perhaps because I am shorter than just about everyone else and they can relate to my efforts to be as good as bigger players.

I've written about the Japanese fans earlier in the book, how they cheered Mum and me when we embraced in the stands after my debut for the Matildas in 2012. There were almost weekly reminders of their role when I played club football in Tokyo, particularly in home games where players would be presented with gifts as we were leaving the ground.

They were mostly tokens of esteem, treat bags filled with home-made sweets and buns, although on occasions the gifts were more valuable, like the time my team-mate Caitlin Foord was given a Louis Vuitton bag.

At home games with Brisbane Roar I had a special friend in the crowd. Rory has Down Syndrome like Dylan, although they don't know each other, and we established a special bond. I would go over after each game to get a hug from him, no matter what had happened in the match.

As players, we can also have a big impact in people's lives outside the joy of watching a game.

One of my favourite moments came when I was doing a fan meet-and-greet at West Ham. A young woman standing in line looked very nervous as she approached and told me: 'I don't think you realise the impact you've had on my life. Thank you.' And with that she walked off.

I was stunned and when I saw her standing nearby later, I signalled that I wanted to talk more to her. She told me her name and that she was gay. 'I have struggled with my sexuality,' she said. 'Coming out was really, really hard for me. Then I found out about you and how you raised Harper. It inspired me and helped me get out of a really dark place. I'll never know how to repay you.'

By the time she had finished we were both crying and I felt as joyful as if I had just raised the World Cup over my head—well, almost.